Handprint Quilts

Creating Children's Keepsakes with Paint and Fabric

Marcia L. Layton

Martingale™
& COMPANY

Credits

President	Nancy J. Martin
CEO	Daniel J. Martin
Publisher	Jane Hamada
Editorial Director	Mary V. Green
Managing Editor	Tina Cook
Technical Editor	Dawn Anderson
Copy Editor	Erana Bumbardatore
Design Director	Stan Green
Illustrator	Laurel Strand
Text Designer	Regina Girard
Cover Designer	Stan Green
Photographer	Brent Kane

That Patchwork Place® is an imprint of Martingale & Company™.

Handprint Quilts:
Creating Children's Keepsakes with Paint and Fabric
© 2003 by Marcia L. Layton

Martingale & Company
20205 144th Avenue NE
Woodinville, WA 98072-8478 USA
www.martingale-pub.com

Printed in China
08 07 06 05 04 03   8 7 6 5 4 3 2 1

Mission Statement

We are dedicated to providing quality products and service by working together to inspire creativity and to enrich the lives we touch.

Library of Congress Cataloging-in-Publication Data
Turner, Marcia Layton.
    Handprint quilts : creating children's keepsakes with paint and fabric / Marcia L. Layton.
        p. cm.
    ISBN 1-56477-458-9
    1. Textile painting. 2. Patchwork. 3. Machine appliqué.
I. Title.
TT851 .T87 2002
746.46—dc21   2002151275

Dedication

To my parents, Annie and Fred Stumme, who have given me their love and support all my life, and to my children, Melissa, Tommy, Robert, and Carrie. Without their encouragement, patience, and wonderful help, I would not have been able to begin to realize this dream.

Acknowledgments

I would like to say thank you to:

All of the children at Play Haven Preschool in Tampa, who over the years have so enriched my life and lent many little hands to my quilts.

My dear friends and fellow teachers Betsy Sanders, Sue Johnston, Ruth Toro, and Sue Gandy, who encouraged me to try out my ideas and patiently helped me print all of those little hands.

The families who lent their school auction quilts to me for the book.

The Morris family girls—Isabelle, Olivia, and their mother, Ruth—who were always ready to lend a hand, literally!

My friend and fellow quilter, Michele Heitlinger, whose energy and enthusiasm never failed to inspire me.

My dearest friend, Suzanne Crosby, who offered encouragement when I needed it most.

Ditto Gutcher, who patiently answered my questions when I was just starting to think about publishing.

Author Mischele Hart, who graciously shared her knowledge and encouragement along the way.

Martingale & Company and all of the staff who have given me this exciting opportunity to share my ideas.

Contents

Introduction

About four years ago, I made my first handprint quilt. It was very simple, made by printing children's hands on squares of colored fabric. I cut the prints out and appliquéd them by hand with a buttonhole stitch to a white muslin square. Then I framed the square with a wonderful printed fabric of children's happy faces. At the time, I was the teacher of a lively group of four-year-olds, and the quilt was my way of creating a memento of their preschool year.

The skills needed to make the quilt were basic and both the time investment and expense were minimal. Otherwise, I probably never would have attempted it because I was by no means an experienced quilter. But I made it and as they say, the rest is history! I enjoyed making that first quilt so much that the next school year another version, a handprint garden, followed. Handprint ideas started popping into my head and multiplying, and over the next two years I made seven more little quilts with hands. Once I started thinking of all of the handprint design possibilities and of combining these with all of the wonderful novelty prints and other fabrics available, I couldn't stop.

I shared my ideas with friends and other quilters, and I was excited to see that they were interested in using the designs to make their own wonderful keepsakes. This book is a result of the true enjoyment that has come from sharing these quilts with others.

Handprint Quilts was written to take the trial and error out of creating personal handprint quilts. The first part of the book details the supplies needed and the process of printing on fabric with hands, plus suggestions for embellishing the handprints in a variety of ways. A section on constructing and finishing the quilts follows, plus a special section offering tips on planning your own handprint quilt. The project section includes a number of handprint quilts, each of which can be varied a number of ways.

Handprint quilts are quite simple to make, and the choice of embellishment is up to the quilter. There is a lot of fun involved in the painting and printing of little hands, and even adults get inspired when making their personal prints for a quilt. Such has been my experience, and I hope that everyone who reads this book will enjoy making these quilts as much as I have!

Creating a Handprint Quilt

Supplies

Fabric. Use good-quality white or unbleached muslin for the printed areas. Wash the fabric and iron it smooth before printing. For the rest of the quilt, you can combine the fabrics of your choice. There are many delightful novelty prints that can give your handprint quilt a special theme that's reflected in your handprint design. For quilts that are primarily decorative, cottons, cotton blends, and synthetics can be successfully combined. The simplicity of the quilts also makes it possible to use different kinds of fabrics.

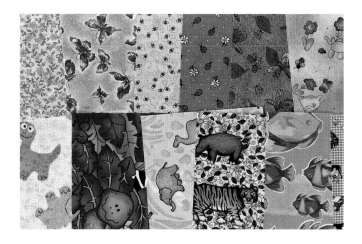

This is just a sampling of the wide range of fabric patterns available to combine with your handprint pieces.

Rotary cutter, ruler, and mat. These are used for cutting quilt blocks, sashings, and borders.

Scissors. Use scissors to cut ribbons and other embellishments.

Water-based acrylic craft paints. These paints come in many colors and brands. They can easily be mixed to create additional colors.

Fabric or textile medium. This liquid is usually found in craft stores right next to the acrylic paints. It can be mixed with regular acrylic paint to transform it into fabric paint.

Craft brushes. These are used to paint the children's hands, and you'll need several different sizes. Inexpensive brushes like those used for children's poster paints and watercolors work well.

Paper towels or moistened wipes. Use these for wiping paint off hands.

Containers for mixing paint. I use empty Styrofoam egg cartons and trays, and even paper plates to hold my paint.

Cardboard or heavy paper. This is to put under your fabric as you create your handprints. I like to use cut-up brown grocery bags or pieces of cardboard. The fabric can then be taped down to the paper. It also helps to slip a small piece of plastic wrap or a cut-up plastic bag between the fabric and the paper to keep the paint from sticking as it dries.

Masking tape. This is used to secure fabric squares to a surface before printing.

Fabric glues. Special glues are available for attaching ribbon, fringes, and other trims to the quilt. Other types are made especially for attaching googly eyes, beads, gemstones, and other materials.

Fray Check. This is important to use on the ends of ribbons and cut areas of trim to prevent fraying.

Embellishments. Embroidery floss, decorative threads, ribbons, rickrack, fringe, sequins, bells, googly eyes, dimensional paint, glitter, and fabric markers can be used to decorate your quilt.

Thread. Mercerized cotton or cotton-polyester thread is used for quilt construction and machine quilting. Invisible nylon thread can also be used for machine quilting. Hand-quilting thread is used for hand-quilted areas.

Pins. You'll need long quilter's pins and 1" nickel-plated safety pins to pin-baste your quilt for sewing and quilting.

Assorted needles, thimble, and an embroidery hoop. You'll need these for your embroidery and hand quilting.

Sewing machine. You don't need a fancy sewing machine for these quilts. Any model with a good straight stitch will do.

Assorted sewing machine feet. A foot that measures exactly ¼" from the center needle position to the edge of the foot makes accurate piecing easy. And a walking foot for straight-line quilting is recommended, but it's not absolutely necessary.

Low-loft polyester or cotton batting. Low-loft batting is preferred for both hand and machine quilting.

Printing the Quilt

Printing a handprint quilt is not a difficult process, but it does involve some advance preparation and planning. Along with a willing handprint artist, you will need a flat, protected work surface and access to a sink to wash the paint off afterward. Keep a supply of paper towels or moistened wipes nearby.

To begin printing, you will need muslin fabric that has been washed and ironed flat. This should be cut or torn to the desired size of your finished square or panel, plus 2 inches. (The extra inches allow you to trim the piece and nicely center your design after printing.) Before you actually paint, it helps to practice placing the printer's hand on the fabric to decide exactly where you want it to be. With young children, you will need to show them exactly how you want them to put their fingers down, whether spread apart or held together. Practice this a few times. Urge them to let you move their hand and not to move a finger until so directed.

Start by taping the fabric to a piece of heavy paper or cardboard for support. I also like to slip a little piece of plastic wrap or a cut-up plastic bag between the fabric and the paper, to prevent the paint from sticking as it dries. Set this aside.

Pour a small amount of paint into a small container. If you need to mix colors to get the exact shade you need for your print, you can do that here. Then add about an equal amount of fabric medium to your paint. (Don't make your paint too thin; just aim for a nice painting consistency. You don't want it to drip off the child's hands.) If for some reason you can't find this

medium at the store—I sometimes have this problem—you can still make prints with the regular acrylic paint. Your prints will be a little stiffer and the paint will dry much more quickly on the hand as you print, though, so you will need to work fast to get the best results.

For some handprints, you will use just one color. (This is especially recommended when you are printing with very small children.) At other times, you might choose to combine several colors in a print. In those cases, have all of your paints for the handprint ready at one time. You can carefully paint each section of the hand the desired color and print in one motion. For some prints with small spots or stripes or blended colors, you can apply a base color and then just dab the other colors on top before printing.

Once your paint is ready, work over a covered area (I usually have several paper towels underneath the hand I'm painting, to catch drips and splatters), and fill your brush with paint. Holding the printer's hand palm side up, paint the hand as desired. Work quickly and cover all areas with an even coat of paint. The painting tickles, so you will probably hear a few giggles from your handprint artist.

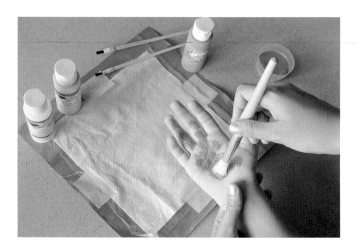

Then carefully move over to your piece of fabric, turn the hand over, and place it where desired. Press each finger from the tip toward the palm and at each joint. Press down firmly on the printer's palm. (You usually get some paint on your own hands while doing this, so be careful not to get it on the fabric.)

Next, carefully lift the hand. Sometimes the fabric will try to pull up as well. The tape will help keep it in place, but you will probably have to pull the fabric down too. Again, be careful not to accidentally touch any paint from your hands to the fabric.

To avoid having paint end up where you don't want it, paint only one hand at a time. Immediately after printing, send your printer straight to the sink to wash up. With young children, it is best to hold their wrist all the way to the sink and help them wash!

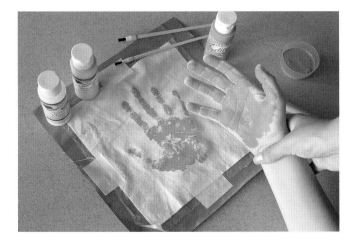

Set the handprint aside to dry. The paint will be dry to the touch in less than an hour.

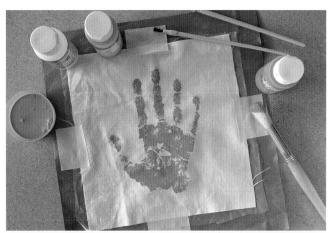

Remove the tape and lift the fabric from the paper and plastic to allow it to finish drying. It will later need to be heat-set with an iron. The brand of textile medium that you use will determine the length of time to wait before heat-setting and ironing. Follow the directions for your particular brand, and iron while using a press cloth over the unpainted side of your fabric.

Embellishing the Quilt

After your printing is done and the handprints have dried and been heat-set, trim the printed piece to the desired size, centering the print nicely. You are now ready to start embellishing your print. Most of the embellishment is done before the quilt top is constructed, unless a particular embellishment will be too close to a seam line and will interfere with later sewing and machine quilting.

When embellishing your prints, you are limited only by your imagination and the materials you have available. Embroidery is a wonderful way to create handprint features. It is best worked in a hoop, taking care not to pull too hard on the painted print, to avoid distorting it. It can be difficult to pull thread through thicker areas of paint, so a thimble will come in handy at times. It is also important to plan carefully where you will embroider, because the paint does not forgive mistakes very well. Needle holes will show, if you have to rip out stitches.

The following embroidery stitches are used for the designs shown in this book.

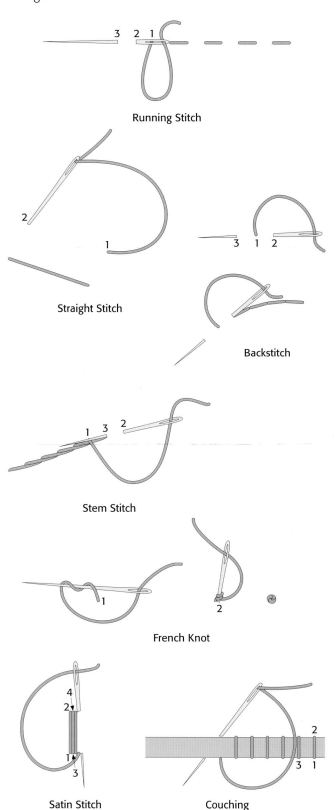

Running Stitch

Straight Stitch

Backstitch

Stem Stitch

French Knot

Satin Stitch

Couching

Dimensional fabric paint is another fun way to bring handprints to life. It comes in many bright and glittery colors and can create interesting designs and textures on the prints. Fabric markers can be used to personalize handprints and to add features as well.

To add even more interest to handprints, you can use permanent glues to attach trims to your quilt. Beads, bells, braids, buttons, googly eyes, feathers, fringes, fusible appliqués, ribbons, sequins, and tiny resin figures are all items that I have used successfully. Finding the perfect accessories to complete these quilts is half the fun!

Your printed quilt can be washed as long as the embellishments you use are washable. For best results, limit the embellishments to embroidery, buttons, fabric trims, or dimensional paint if the quilt is to be laundered. Anything secured with fabric glue might come unglued during washing, depending on the type of glue you use. Be sure to stitch trims in place.

Note: When making quilts for small children, limit embellishments to embroidery or dimensional paint. Other small embellishments could pose a choking hazard for young children.

Constructing and Finishing the Quilt

After the handprints have been printed and embellished, you're ready to assemble your quilt top. Sew sashing and borders to the muslin handprint blocks and panels with ¼" seams. Refer to "Adding Borders," below, to add straight-cut borders to your quilt. Then finish the quilt with either binding or rickrack edging, as described on pages 9–10.

Adding Borders

The quilts in this book all have simple straight-edge borders. The lengths of the border strips are listed in the cutting directions for each project. However, if the quilt top has many seams, you may wish to measure the actual top before cutting the border strips to ensure that the strips will fit the quilt. Stretching can occur during construction, causing the edges of the quilt top to measure longer than the length through the center of the quilt, and seams sewn wider than ¼" can cause a quilt top to "shrink." If you decide to measure your quilt top, do it through the center in both directions and cut the border strips to the measured lengths. You can cut border strips on the crosswise grain of the fabric and piece them to be as long as necessary. I choose not to piece my borders and therefore have to cut the longer border strips from the lengthwise grain of the fabric.

Finishing with Binding

Make a quilt sandwich by layering the backing (right side down, taped to a flat, smooth surface), the batting, and the quilt top (right side up). Pin-baste the layers of fabric and batting together using #2 rustproof safety pins spaced every 6" to 8" throughout the quilt; then remove the tape.

With a walking foot on your sewing machine, quilt by stitching "in the ditch" along the seam line around each handprint square or panel, working from the center of the quilt out toward the edges. Follow the quilting directions given for each project to add further quilting to your handprint quilt. After quilting, trim the batting and backing even witht he edges of the quilt top.

Bind the quilt with French double-fold binding, cutting 2"-wide binding strips across the width of the fabric. Sew the binding strips together as described below, to equal the measurement of the perimeter of the quilt, plus 10".

1. Join strips with their right sides together and at right angles. Trim ¼" from the stitching and press the seam allowances open.

binding strips. Pin the binding strips to the front of the quilt top along the side edges, matching pin marks and ends. Sew in place using a ¼" seam allowance. Fold the binding to the back of the quilt and blind-stitch in place, just covering the stitching line.

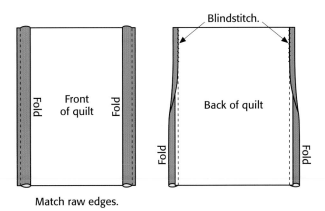

Match raw edges.

3. Measure the quilt top horizontally through the center and cut 2 binding strips to that measurement, plus 1". Fold the strips in half lengthwise, wrong sides together, and press. Pin-mark the center of the quilt top along the top and bottom edges and pin-mark the centers of the binding strips. Pin the binding strips to the front of the quilt top along the top and bottom edges, matching pin marks and allowing the binding to extend ½" beyond each end. Sew in place, using a ¼" seam allowance. Fold in the ends; then fold the binding to the back of the quilt and blindstitch in place, just covering the stitching line.

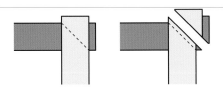

Joining Straight-Cut Strips

2. Measure the quilt top vertically through the center and cut 2 binding strips to that measurement. Fold the strips in half lengthwise, wrong sides together, and press. Pin-mark the center of the quilt top along the side edges and pin-mark the centers of the

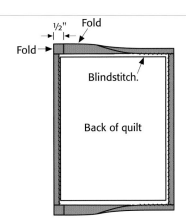

Finishing with Rickrack Edging

Before you make your quilt sandwich (backing, batting, and quilt top), sew the rickrack along the edge of the quilt top, centering the trim ¼" from the raw edges. (This is exactly where your seam line will fall when you sew your quilt together.) It is easier to cut a separate piece of trim for each side than it is to try and go around the corners with one long piece. For neat corners, make sure that the rickrack tapers off (ends with a valley rather than a hump) at the corners.

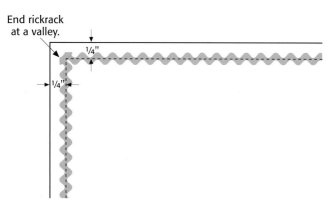

End rickrack at a valley.

¼"

¼"

Center and sew rickrack ¼" from raw edges.

Layer the quilt with the batting first, then the backing fabric (right side up), and then the quilt top (right side down). Stitch ¼" from the outer edges using the stitching line from the rickrack as a guide, and leave an opening about 18" long on one edge. Turn the quilt right side out through the opening and slipstitch the opening closed.

Pin-baste the layers of fabric and batting together with rustproof safety pins, spacing the pins 6" to 8" apart. With a walking foot on your sewing machine, quilt by stitching "in the ditch" along the seam line around each handprint square or panel, working from the center of the quilt out toward the edges. Add further quilting to your handprint quilt by following any additional quilting directions given for your project.

Labeling the Quilt

For a finishing touch, add a quilt label to the back of your quilt with your name, the date, the place, and any other special information about the quilt. Be sure to include the names of your handprint artists and their ages, if they are children. To make a label, simply write the desired information on a small rectangle of fabric using a permanent-ink pen. Turn under the raw edges and hand-stitch the label to the back of your quilt.

Tips for Planning Your Own Quilt

Each quilt in this book is as unique as the hands that printed it. When you plan your own handprint quilt, you'll need to consider many things, such as the number of hands you are printing, the age of your handprint artist(s), and the size you want your finished quilt to be. Other factors, such as the fabrics you want to use, the trims available, and your personal preferences, will also affect your planning decisions.

When I plan a handprint quilt, I first consider the number and size of hands I am printing. Most of my quilts are used as decorative wall hangings, so the finished quilt size is a factor, too. For a single block, I will look at the largest handprint, decide how much white background is desirable, and set my block size from that measurement. If I am printing a number of hands that can be displayed in even rows, I usually decide to proceed with even rows of individual blocks, set apart with sashing. However, if I am printing a large number of hands that if printed individually would result in a very large quilt, I will opt to print panels where the prints can be placed closer together. Panels also work well if the number of handprints is uneven. The only drawback to panels is that extra care must be taken while printing, since one "misprint" can ruin the whole panel.

The age of your artist is also important to consider when you are planning the complexity of the prints. Single, one-color prints work best for very young children. Children this age usually don't have the patience or control for extensive painting and exact positioning of their hands. They do enjoy the process, however.

Once you decide how you wish to print the hands, you'll need to assemble your border fabrics and some of the trims to complete your design. Your own preferences and the availability of these items are the guideline factors. Since most of these quilts are not really designed to be washable, you can get creative in your choices of fabrics and trims. These choices will in turn influence the choice of colors for the handprints.

Each quilt design in this book is different because of one or more of the considerations mentioned here. Each design can be enlarged or reduced simply by adding blocks or adjusting the block size, and then adjusting the borders using some simple math. As you look through each quilt project, you'll find that I've included notes and suggestions for how to resolve some of the design problems you might encounter. Happy handprinting!

Handprint Quilt Gallery

Jungle Flowers by Michele Heitlinger, 35" x 55". Printed by Ms. Lynn and her kindergarten class at Mitchell Elementary School, Tampa, Florida. (From the collection of Michelle Shimberg.)

These handprints, embellished with rickrack and buttons,
take on the vivid colors of the jungle-print border.

Grandma's Birthday Quilt
by Marcia L. Layton, 52½" x 52½".
Printed by the Layton family. (From
the collection of Georgette Layton.)

*Each grandchild printed a colorful
butterfly to complete this memory quilt.
A black embroidery-floss running stitch,
inspired by the border fabric, adds
interest to the butterfly wings. Most of
these prints were made by teenagers!
To print the butterflies, refer to "Beautiful
Butterflies" on pages 27–29.*

Garden of Friends by Marcia L. Layton, 50" x 35". Printed by Marcia L. Layton and her class of
four-year-olds at Play Haven Preschool, Tampa, Florida. (From the collection of Jenny Carey.)

*This panel of long-stemmed handprint flowers is embellished with tiny fingerprint ladybugs, ants,
caterpillars, and bumblebees. Refer to "Flower Garden" on pages 24–26 for general directions.*

Steven's Dinosaur by Marcia L. Layton, 16" x 16".
Printed by five-year-old Steven Centeno.
(From the collection of the Centeno family.)

Dinosaur-print border fabric complements this dinosaur handprint. To print the Dinosaur block, follow the directions for "Dinosaur Days" on pages 44–50.

Caroline's Flower by Marcia L. Layton, 16" x 16".
Printed by two-year-old Caroline Centeno.
(From the collection of the Centeno family.)

To print the flower, refer to the directions for "Flower Garden" on pages 24–26. The fingerprint ladybug and bee are embellished with embroidery stitches.

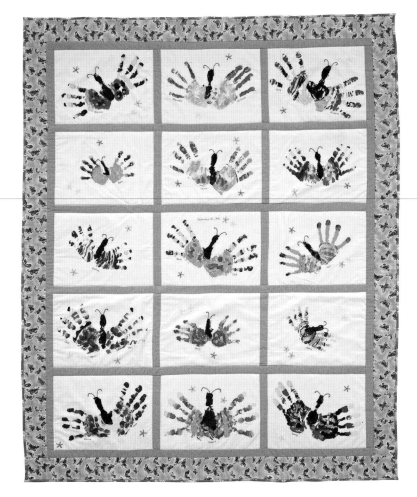

Mom and Dad's Anniversary Quilt
by Marcia L. Layton, 50½" x 62".
Printed by the Stumme family. (From the collection of the Stumme family.)

Four generations are represented in this butterfly quilt. While the young grandchildren and great-grandchildren each printed individual butterflies, their parents printed matching halves to make up the blocks. On the butterflies, iridescent sequins provide sparkle. To print the butterflies, refer to the directions for "Beautiful Butterflies" on pages 27–29.

Maranda's Butterfly by Marcia L. Layton, 16" x 16".
Printed by four-year-old Maranda Centeno.
(From the collection of the Centeno family.)

*A bright butterfly flutters in the center of this pillow.
To print the Butterfly block, refer to the directions
for "Beautiful Butterflies" on pages 27–29.*

Chicken Scratch by Marcia L. Layton, 14" x 14".
Printed by two-year-old Olivia Morris.

*One little chicken makes tracks across the square of this
simple country pillow. To print the Chicken block, refer to
the directions for "Just Us Chickens" on pages 60–63.*

Sunflower by Michele Heitlinger, 19" x 43½". Printed by
Ms. Carrigan and her pre-K class at Mitchell Elementary
School, Tampa, Florida. (From the collection of Janet King.)

*This bright flower panel, embellished with buttons and bows,
is made with the handprints of an entire class! To print the
sunflower, refer to the directions for "Busy Bees and
Sunflower" on pages 30–33.*

It's Raining Cats and Dogs
by Marcia L. Layton, 18" x 18". Printed by Tess, Emily, and Anna Stumme. (From the collection of the Stumme family.)

Handprint dogs and novelty buttons are the perfect match for this "rainy" animal print. To print the dogs, refer to the directions for "Dalmatians Everywhere!" on pages 40–43.

Butterflies and Flowers
by Marcia L. Layton, 37" x 46". Printed by Betsy Sanders, Ruth Toro, Sue Johnston, and the classes of two-year-olds at Play Haven Preschool, Tampa, Florida. (From the collection of the Heiny family.)

Alternating panels of flowers and butterflies are printed in vivid colors and embellished with buttons that match the flowers and butterflies of the border print.

Happy Hands

By Marcia L. Layton, 27 ½" x 38". Printed by Carrie Layton.

Brightly colored handprints smile amid the colors of a lively happy-face fabric.

Materials

Yardage is based on 42"-wide fabric.

¾ yd. of muslin for blocks

⅛ yd. *each* of 6 bright colors for block borders (aqua, lime green, orange, pink, purple, and yellow)

⅝ yd. of happy-face print for outer border

1⅜ yds. of multicolor print for backing and binding

32" x 42" piece of low-loft batting

Acrylic paints: aqua, blue, orange, pink, red, and yellow

Black dimensional fabric paint

Fabric	Pieces to Cut
Muslin	6 squares, 10½" x 10½"
Each bright color (aqua, lime green, orange, pink, purple, and yellow)	2 strips, 1¾" x 8½" 2 strips, 1¾" x 11"
Happy-face print	2 strips, 3½" x 27½" 2 strips, 3½" x 32"
Multicolor print	4 strips, 2" x 42" 1 piece, 32" x 42"

Making the Handprint Blocks

Refer to "Printing the Quilt" on page 6. Use the quilt photo on page 16 as a guide for the placement of the painted features.

1. Print a different color handprint in each of the 6 muslin squares, printing the hand with the fingers slightly spread. Print some squares using the left hand and some using the right, using the quilt photo as a guide. Heat-set the handprints, following the manufacturer's directions.
2. Use the black dimensional fabric paint to paint 2 black dots for eyes and a happy smile across the palm of each hand.
3. Trim the squares to 8½" x 8½", centering each handprint.

Constructing the Quilt

All measurements include ¼"-wide seam allowances unless otherwise noted.

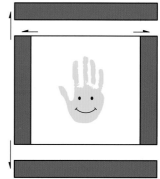

1. Referring to the quilt photo for color combinations, sew matching 1¾" x 8½" bright-color strips to the sides of the handprint blocks. Then sew the matching 1¾" x 11" bright strips to the tops and bottoms of the blocks.

Make 6.

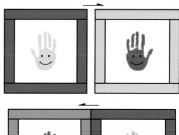

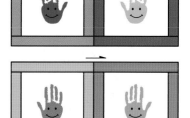

2. Arrange the blocks in 3 rows of 2 blocks each, as shown. Sew the blocks together in horizontal rows.
3. Sew the rows together.
4. Sew the 3½" x 32" happy-face border strips to the sides of the quilt top. Press the seams toward the border. Sew the 3½" x 27½" happy-face border strips to the top and bottom of the quilt. Press the seams toward the border.
5. Referring to "Finishing with Binding" on page 9, construct the quilt sandwich, pin-baste, and machine quilt along the seam lines. Bind the edges of the quilt and add a label to the back.

Design Tip

It's easy to enlarge this quilt by simply adding blocks. Using school colors would make the quilt a great classroom project, and to make it extra special, each child could write his or her name in a block and draw a face on the painted handprint.

Sweet Hearts

By Marcia L. Layton, 39½" x 39½". Printed by Carrie Layton.

Bright pastel handprint hearts combine with a colorful heart border to say, "I love you!"

Materials

Yardage is based on 42"-wide fabric.

1⅛ yds. of muslin for blocks

¾ yd. of pink check for sashing and inner border

½ yd. of heart print for outer border

1⅜ yds. of fabric for backing

⅜ yd. of blue print for binding

44" x 44" piece of low-loft batting

Acrylic paints: aqua, blue, pink, and yellow

Four 1" heart-shaped buttons

White hand-quilting thread

Fabric	Pieces to Cut
Muslin	9 squares, 11½" x 11½"
Pink check	6 strips, 2" x 9½" 4 strips, 2" x 30½" 2 strips, 2" x 33½"
Heart print	2 strips, 3½" x 33½" 2 strips, 3½" x 39½"
Blue print	5 strips, 2" x 42"
Backing	1 square, 44" x 44"

Making the Handprint Blocks

Refer to "Printing the Quilt" on page 6.

1. With 2 straight pins, mark the center top and bottom of a square of muslin. Use these pins as guides for placing the handprints.
2. Print the right hand in about the vertical center of the square, at a 45° angle to the imaginary centerline between the pins, with the fingers and thumb held close together. The fingers should point in toward the center of the square, and the ends of the thumb and middle finger should fall on your imaginary centerline.

Note: The handprints are printed with the fingers pointing up and away from the printer. After printing, the squares are turned upside down.

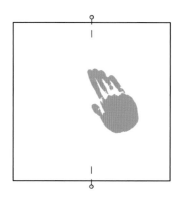

3. Repeat the process with the left hand, printing at the same angle on the other side of the centerline. The tips of the thumb and the middle finger should overlap the fingertips of the right handprint. Print a total of 9 squares in the same manner. Print 3 pink hearts, 2 blue hearts, 2 aqua hearts, and 2 yellow hearts. Heat-set the handprints, following the manufacturer's directions.

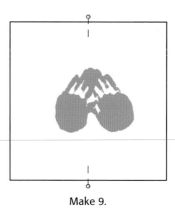

Make 9.

4. Turn the squares upside down to see the hearts. Trim the squares to 9½" x 9½", centering the hearts.

Constructing the Quilt

All measurements include ¼"-wide seam allowances unless otherwise noted.

1. Referring to the photo for color placement, join 3 blocks with 2 strips of 2" x 9½" pink check sashing, as shown. Repeat 2 more times to make 3 units of 3 blocks each.

Make 3.

2. Sew 2 strips of 2" x 30½" pink check sashing between the 3-block units.

3. Sew the 2" x 30½" pink check borders to the sides of the quilt top. Press the seams toward the borders. Sew the 2" x 33½" pink check borders to the top and bottom edges of the quilt. Press the seams toward the borders.

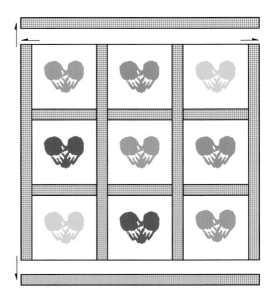

4. Sew the 3½" x 33½" heart-print outer-border strips to the sides of the quilt top. Press the seams toward the border. Sew the 3½" x 39½" heart-print outer-border strips to the top and bottom of the quilt. Press the seams toward the border.

5. Referring to "Finishing with Binding" on page 9, construct the quilt sandwich, pin-baste, and machine quilt along the seam lines.

6. Photocopy the heart quilting pattern on page 21, enlarging it or reducing it as necessary to fit the handprints. Cut it out on the line. Pin the pattern over a heart handprint and use white hand-quilting thread to hand quilt around the outer edges of the pattern. Repeat for the remaining heart prints.

7. Sew the 4 heart buttons in the center of the sashing at the 4 corners of the center heart block.

8. Referring to "Finishing with Binding" on page 9, bind the edges of the quilt. Add a label to the back.

Design Tip

A heart quilt makes a perfect Mother's Day, Valentine's Day, or anniversary gift. Each heart can be printed by one person or two, and then embellished with paint or embroidery.

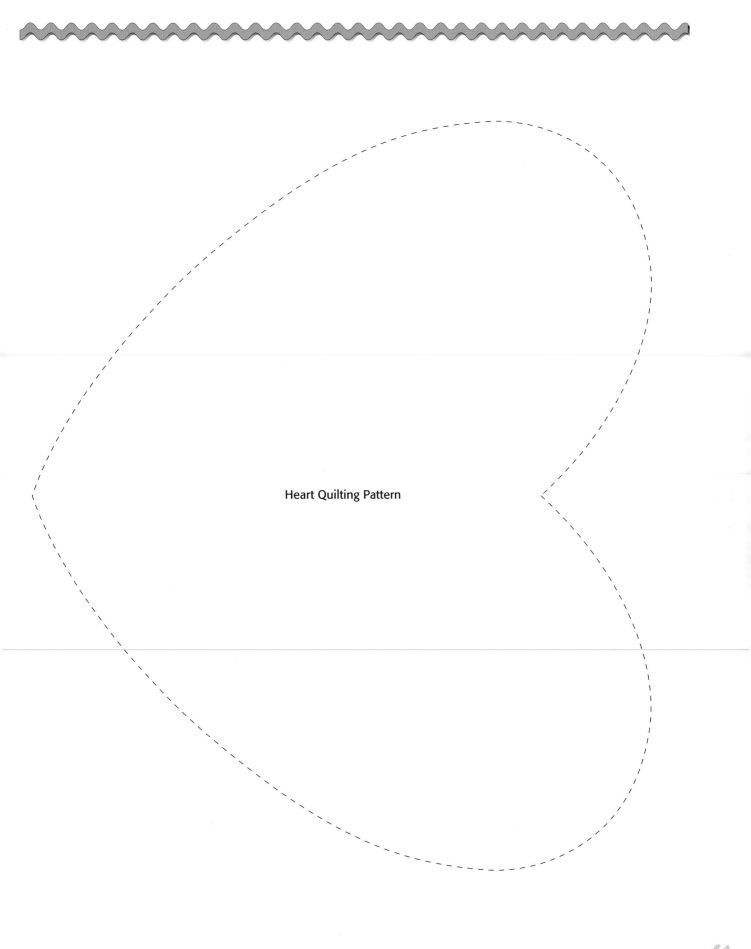

Heart Quilting Pattern

Sweet-Heart Framed Print

By Marcia L. Layton, 17" x 17". Printed by Carrie Layton.

A simple heart-shaped handprint is framed with a dainty pink floral print.

Materials

Yardage is based on 42"-wide fabric.

¾ yd. of white muslin for block and backing

½ yd. of floral print for border

Acrylic paint: pink

Black permanent fabric marker

Pink hand-quilting thread

Fabric	Pieces to Cut
Muslin	1 square, 11½" x 11½"
	1 square, 24" x 24"
Floral print	2 strips, 6" x 9½"
	2 strips, 6" x 20½"

Making the Handprint Block

Refer to "Printing the Quilt" on page 6.

Note: The size of the finished quilt measures 20½" x 20½". I purposely cut the borders extra wide (6") so that the professional framer could pull some of the border fabric to the back of the mounting board during the framing process. This reduced the framed print to 17" x 17".

1. With 2 straight pins, mark the center top and bottom of the 11½" square of muslin. Use these pins as guides for placing the handprints.
2. Print the right hand in about the vertical center of the square, at a 45° angle to the imaginary centerline between the pins, with the fingers and thumb held close together. The fingers should point in toward the center of the square, and the ends of the thumb and middle finger should fall on your imaginary centerline.

   Note: The handprints are printed with the fingers pointing up and away from the printer. After printing, the square is turned upside down.

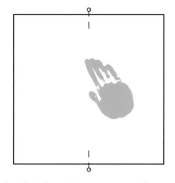

3. Repeat the process with the left hand, printing at the same angle on the other side of the centerline. The tips of the thumb and the middle finger should

overlap the fingertips of the right handprint.

4. Turn the print upside down to see the heart. Using the fabric marker, write the printer's name to the lower right of the heart print. Heat-set the handprints, following the manufacturer's directions.

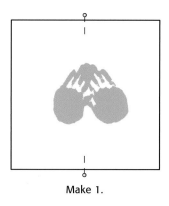

Make 1.

5. Trim the square to 9½" x 9½".

Constructing the Quilt

1. Sew the 6" x 9½" floral-print strips to the top and bottom of the quilt block. Press the seams toward the strips. Sew the 6" x 20½" floral-print strips to the sides of the quilt block. Press the seams toward the strips.

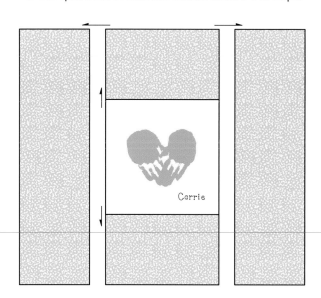

Carrie

2. Referring to "Finishing with Binding" on page 9, construct the quilt sandwich, pin-baste, and machine quilt along the seam lines.
3. Photocopy the heart quilting pattern on page 21, enlarging it or reducing it as necessary to fit the handprints. Cut it out on the line. Pin the pattern over the heart print and use pink hand-quilting thread to hand quilt around the outer edges of the pattern. Remove the pattern.
4. Trim the batting and backing even with the edges of the quilt top. Leave the outside edges unfinished. The block is ready to be professionally framed.

Flower Garden

By Annie L. Stumme, 30½" x 23". Designed by Marcia L. Layton and printed
by the William Stumme family. (From the collection of the Stumme family.)

Each family member's handprint becomes a pretty spring flower in this quilted garden.

Materials

Yardage is based on 42"-wide fabric.

¾ yd. of muslin for printed panel

½ yd. of floral print for borders

1 yd. of fabric for backing

27" x 34½" piece of low-loft batting

Acrylic paints: blue, fuchsia, orange, pink, red, and yellow

Green rayon thread

¾ yd. of ⅝"-wide green ribbon

1⅝ yds. of ¼"-wide green ribbon

2 purchased iron-on bumblebees

1 purchased iron-on butterfly

Black embroidery floss

⅞ yd. of green rickrack, large sized

3 yds. of blue rickrack, medium sized

Fabric	Pieces to Cut
Muslin	1 rectangle, 19" x 26½"
Floral print	2 strips, 3½" x 17" 2 strips, 3½" x 30½"
Backing	1 rectangle, 27" x 34½"

Making the Handprint Panel

Refer to "Printing the Quilt" on page 6 and "Embellishing the Quilt" on pages 7–8. Use the quilt photo on page 24 as a guide for the placement of the embroidery stitches and embellishments. Refer to the embroidery stitches on page 8 and use 3 strands of embroidery floss for the stitches.

1. To determine the placement of the handprints, use pins to mark the center of each edge of the muslin panel. Also place a pin at each corner 1" in from the sides to mark off the trimmed panel dimmensions (17" x 24½"). The extra inches in your panel allow you some room for adjustment if you do get things off-center while printing. Practice placing hands on the fabric until you get a pleasing arrangement and even spacing. Place a pin just below the spot where you want each print to be.

2. Once your fabric is marked, print 5 different colored hands. Print some right hands and some left hands, and stagger the prints to fill the space. Refer to the quilt photo for color placement and positioning. Heat-set the handprints, following the manufacturer's directions.

3. Use your sewing machine and the green rayon thread to sew a length of ⅝"-wide green ribbon from the base of each handprint to the bottom of the panel. Tie 5 bows, using about 11" of ¼"-wide green ribbon for each, and tack them to the tops of the ribbon "stems."

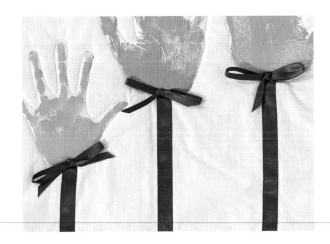

4. Referring to the quilt photo, fuse the iron-on insects in place, following the manufacturer's directions. With a running stitch and black embroidery floss, create looped trails behind the bees.

5. Sew a piece of large green rickrack across the bottom of the panel so that the bottom of the trim falls slightly more than ¼" from the raw edge.

6. With red paint and your index finger, add a finger-print ladybug above the rickrack "grass." Heat-set the print, following the manufacturer's directions. Referring to the embroidery stitches on page 8 and the illustration below, add details to the ladybug with black embroidery floss.

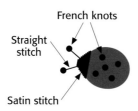

French knots

Straight stitch

Satin stitch

7. Trim the finished panel to 17" x 24½".

Constructing the Quilt

All measurements include ¼"-wide seam allowances unless otherwise noted.

1. Sew the 3½" x 17" floral-print border strips to the sides of the panel. Press the seams toward the border. Sew the 3½" x 30½" floral-print border strips to the top and bottom of the panel. Press the seams toward the border.

2. Refer to "Finishing with Rickrack Edging" on page 10 to construct the quilt sandwich and finish the quilt, using the blue rickrack. Machine quilt along the seam lines and around the flowers. Add a label to the back of the quilt.

Design Tip

This design is wonderfully versatile. The flowers can be printed in any and every color, and each flower can be printed on a single block or as part of a panel. You could vary the height of each panel with the length of the flower stems, and the width could change with the number of flowers and the spacing between prints. To make a larger quilt, just add blocks and panels.

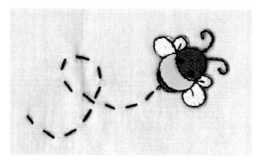

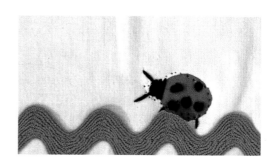

Beautiful Butterflies

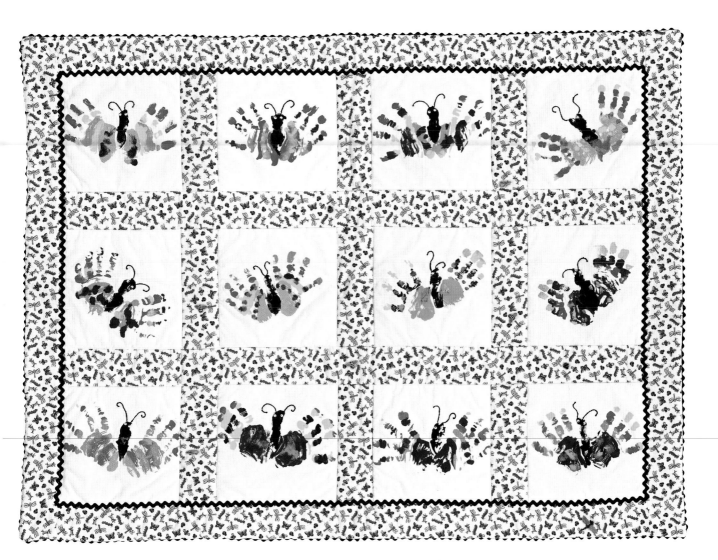

By Marcia L. Layton, 44½" x 34". Printed by Marcia L. Layton and her class of four-year-olds at Play Haven Preschool, Tampa, Florida. (From the collection of the Smith family.)

Multicolor handprint butterflies bring out all of the colors of the insects in this springtime fabric.

Materials

Yardage is based on 42"-wide fabric.

1³⁄₈ yds. of white muslin for blocks

1 yd. of butterfly print for sashing and border

1⁵⁄₈ yds. of fabric for backing

38" x 48" piece of low-loft batting

Acrylic paints: black, dark blue, light blue, green, orange, pink, purple, red, and yellow

Black embroidery floss

Fabric glue

12 pairs of 3 mm googly eyes

8¼ yds. of black rickrack, medium sized

6 resin insects

Fabric	Pieces to Cut
Muslin	12 squares, 10½" x 10½"
Butterfly print	9 strips, 3" x 8½" 4 strips, 3" x 40" 2 strips, 3" x 34½"
Backing	1 rectangle, 38" x 48"

Making the Handprint Blocks

Refer to "Printing the Quilt" on page 6 and "Embellishing the Quilt" on pages 7–8. Use the quilt photo on page 27 as a guide for the placement of the embroidery stitches and embellishments. Refer to the embroidery stitches on page 8 and use 3 strands of embroidery floss for the stitches.

1. Starting with the printer's right hand, paint the thumb black, extending the paint down into the palm area. This forms the butterfly's body. Using the color of your choice, paint the palm of the hand. Then using 3 or 4 other paint colors, add dots and stripes all over the palm and across the fingers. Print the hand on a muslin square, placing the thumb vertically in approximately the center of the square and spreading the fingers out to the side.

2. Paint the left hand to match the right hand. Print this hand by placing the left thumb exactly on top of the thumb print of the right hand and spreading the fingers out to the side.

3. Print a total of 12 different butterflies, varying the colors and the positioning of the hands. Tilt some to the left, others to the right, and print some straight up and down. (Refer to the quilt photo on page 27 for ideas.) Heat-set the handprints, following the manufacturer's directions.

4. Referring to the embroidery stitches on page 8, embroider the butterfly antennae using black embroidery floss and a stem stitch. Make each antenna about 1" long. Curve your stitches around, varying the shape from one butterfly to the next, and end with a French knot.

5. Glue 2 googly eyes in place on each butterfly.

6. Trim the squares to 8½" x 8½".

Constructing the Quilt

All measurements include ¼"-wide seam allowances unless otherwise noted.

1. Sew 4 Butterfly blocks and three 3" x 8½" butterfly-print sashing strips together. Press the seams toward the sashing. Repeat to make 3 rows.

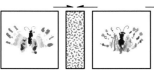

Make 3.

2. Sew the rows together, adding two 3" x 40" butterfly-print sashing strips between them. Press the seams toward the sashing.

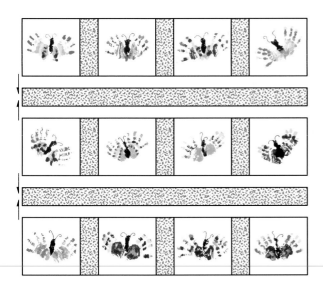

3. Sew two 3" x 40" butterfly-print border strips to the top and bottom of the quilt top. Press the seams toward the border. Sew the 3" x 34½" butterfly-print border strips to the sides of the quilt top. Press the seams toward the border.

4. Referring to "Finishing with Rickrack Edging" on page 10, construct the quilt sandwich and finish the quilt using the black rickrack.

5. Sew black rickrack over the seam between the blocks and the border. Machine quilt along the remaining seam lines.

6. Use the fabric glue to randomly attach the resin insects to the sashing and borders. Add a label to the back of the quilt.

Design Tip

This quilt offers opportunities for several variations. It can be printed with multicolor handprints as shown or with solid-color handprints. Each butterfly can be printed by a single person or by 2 people. This enables you to print either 12 or 24 people's handprints in the same quilt. Blocks like this butterfly design, which use 2 handprints, are larger than blocks with single handprints, but they can be visually appealing.

Busy Bees and Sunflower

By Marcia L. Layton, 43½" x 38". Printed by Sue Gandy and her class of two-year-olds at Play Haven Preschool, Tampa, Florida. (From the collection of the Verdisco family.)

Tiny handprint bees buzz around a large sunflower in this striking black, white, and yellow color combination.

Materials

Yardage is based on 42"-wide fabric.

1⅛ yds. of muslin for blocks and printed panel

⅝ yd. of yellow bee print for sashing and inner border

½ yd. of sunflower print for outer border

1½ yds. of fabric for backing

½ yd. of black solid for binding

42" x 47½" piece of low-loft batting

Acrylic paints: brown, moss green, and golden yellow

Embroidery floss: black, green, and golden yellow

Fabric glue

6 pairs of 3 mm googly eyes

¼ yd. of black tulle

½ yd. of ⅝"-wide moss green ribbon

¾ yd. of 1½"-wide printed sunflower ribbon

3¾ yds. of black rickrack, medium sized

Fabric	Pieces to Cut
Muslin	6 squares, 10½" x 10½" 1 rectangle, 16" x 30½"
Yellow bee print	4 strips, 2½" x 8½" 2 strips, 2½" x 28½" 2 strips, 2½" x 32½" 2 strips, 2½" x 34"
Sunflower print	4 strips, 3¼" x 38"
Backing	1 piece, 42" x 47½"
Black solid	5 strips, 2" x 42"

Making the Handprint Blocks and Panel

Refer to "Printing the Quilt" on page 6 and "Embellishing the Quilt" on pages 7–8. Use the quilt photo on page 30 as guide for placement of the embroidery stitches and embellishments. Refer to the embroidery stitches on page 8 and use 3 strands of embroidery floss for the stitches.

Bee Blocks

1. Using golden yellow paint and printing with the fingers held close together, create a right handprint in the center of each muslin square. Vary the angles of the prints, making some straight and making others tilt to the right or left. After printing, turn the prints so the thumbs are on top for 3 of the bees (left-facing bees) and the thumbs are on the bottom for the other 3 (right-facing bees). Heat-set the handprints, following the manufacturer's directions.

2. Using the quilt photo as a guide, use black embroidery floss and a stem stitch or backstitch (I used both) to embroider a circle on the palm of each handprint for the bees' faces. Following the curve of the head, stitch stripes across the rest of the palm and the fingers, spacing the stripes about ¼" apart. Use the same stitch to form a mouth within the circle of each bee's head. Stitch 2 antennae protruding from the top of the circle, and end each one with a French knot. At the tip of the longest finger, use straight stitches to make a "Y" with a short stem to indicate the stinger.

3. Glue the googly eyes in place.

4. Using the bee wing pattern on page 33, cut 2 ovals from black tulle for each bee (12 ovals total).

5. Pinch 2 tulle ovals together in the middle and sew them to the top of a bee's body with black sewing thread. Repeat with each square.

6. Trim the squares to 8½" x 8½", centering the bees.

Sunflower Panel

1. To position the handprints for the sunflower, use pins to mark the center of the 16" x 30½" panel along the top and bottom edges. Also place a pin at each corner 1" in from the sides to mark off the trimmed panel dimensions (14" x 28½"). The extra inches in your panel allow you some room for adjustment if you do get things off-center while printing. From the center top of the panel, drop down about 2½" and place another pin. This marks the spot where the fingertips of the center-top handprint should fall.

2. Paint the printer's right hand yellow and print the center-top handprint, referring to the project photo for placement. Spread the fingers slightly.

3. Turn the fabric panel upside down. Repaint the printer's right hand yellow. Along the same centerline established in step 1 and about 3" above the first handprint, print the right hand again. (The fingers will point in the opposite direction from the first print.) Use a pin to mark the center of the distance between the 2 handprints. Continue to repaint the right hand and print 2 more handprints on each side of the center prints, printing so the palms end about 1½" from the center pin. Overlap the handprints as necessary and fan the side hands out at about a 60° angle to the center.

4. Paint the fingertip of the printer's index finger with brown paint and print enough dots to completely fill the area between the palms of the handprints. The dots should resemble the seeds of a sunflower.
5. With the sunflower positioned at the top of the panel, glue moss green ribbon in a straight line from the bottom of the lower handprint to the bottom of the panel.
6. Print a moss green handprint on each side of the ribbon (a right handprint on the right and a left handprint on the left) as shown, with fingers slightly

spread apart. Heat-set the handprints, following the manufacturer's directions.
7. Use black embroidery floss to embroider the sunflower seeds with about 75 French knots. With green embroidery floss and a stem stitch, embroider the stems and veins of the leaves.
8. Tie a bow with the printed sunflower ribbon and glue it to where the green ribbon "stem" meets the base of the flower.
9. Trim the sunflower panel to 14" x 28½", making certain that the sunflower is nicely centered.

Constructing the Quilt

All measurements include ¼"-wide seam allowances unless otherwise noted.

1. Join the 3 right-facing bee blocks with two 2½" x 8½" bee-print sashing strips as shown. Press the seams toward the sashing. Repeat with the left-facing bee blocks to make 2 block and sashing units.

Make 2.

2. Join the block and sashing units from step 1 to the center sunflower panel with the 2½" x 28½" bee-print sashing strips. Press the seams toward the sashing.

3. Sew the 2½" x 32½" bee-print inner-border strips to the top and bottom of the quilt top. Press the seams toward the border. Sew the 2½" x 34" bee-print inner-border strips to the sides of the quilt top. Press the seams toward the border.

4. Sew the black rickrack around the edges of the quilt top, centering the rickrack ¼" from the raw edges of the bee-print border as shown on page 10. Cut a separate piece of rickrack for each side, and for neat corners make sure the rickrack tapers off (ends with

a valley rather than a hump) at the corners. Sew two 3¼" x 38" sunflower-print outer-border strips to the top and bottom of the quilt top, using the stitching line from the rickrack as a guide. Press the seams toward the outer border. Sew the remaining two 3¼" x 38" sunflower-print border strips to the sides of the quilt top in the same manner. Press the seams toward the outer border.

5. Referring to "Finishing with Binding" on page 9, construct the quilt sandwich, pin-baste, and machine quilt along the seam lines. Bind the edges of the quilt and add a label to the back.

Design Tip
This design can be expanded to feature the handprints of any number of people. The sunflower can be used alone and printed as a large panel, enabling you to use many different handprints. Lengthening the stem lets you add more hands as leaves. Handprint bees could then be freely positioned on the panel background. For the quilt shown here, I opted to have the teacher print the more complicated sunflower and her 6 little students each print their own Bee block.

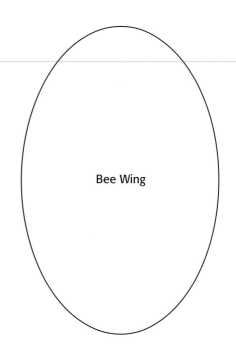

Bee Wing

Busy Bee Pillow

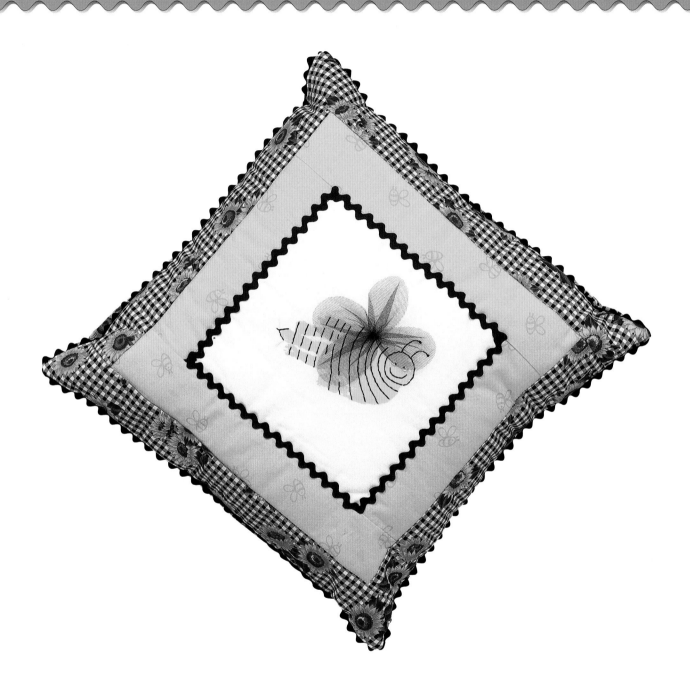

By Marcia L. Layton, 16" x 16". Printed by a four-year-old
at Play Haven Preschool, Tampa, Florida.

A single little bee is framed with rickrack and sunflowers in this bright pillow.

Materials

Yardage is based on 42"-wide fabric.

¾ yd. of muslin for block and backing of quilted pillow top

⅝ yd. of sunflower print for outer border and pillow back

¼ yd. of yellow bee print for inner border

18" x 18" square of low-loft quilt batting

Acrylic paint: golden yellow

Black embroidery floss

Fabric glue

1 pair of 3 mm googly eyes

5" square of black tulle

2⅞ yds. of black rickrack, medium sized

16" x 16" pillow form

Fabric	Pieces to Cut
Muslin	1 square, 10½" x 10½" 1 square, 18" x 18"
Yellow bee print	2 strips, 2½" x 8½" 2 strips, 2½" x 12½"
Sunflower print	2 strips, 2½" x 12½" 2 strips, 2½" x 16½" 2 pieces, 12" x 16½"

Making the Handprint Block

Refer to "Printing the Quilt" on page 6 and "Embellishing the Quilt" on pages 7–8. Use the quilt photo on page 34 as a guide for placement of the embroidery stitches and embellishments. Refer to the embroidery stitches on page 8 and use 3 strands of embroidery floss for the stitches.

1. Using golden yellow paint and printing with the fingers held close together, create a handprint in the center of the 10½" muslin square. Heat-set the handprint, following the manufacturer's directions.

2. Using the photo on page 34 as a guide, use a backstitch or stem stitch and black embroidery floss to embroider a circle on the palm of the handprint for the bee's face (I used a backstitch). Following the curve of the head, stitch stripes across the rest of the palm and the fingers, spacing the stripes about ¼" apart. Use the same stitch to form a mouth within the circle of the bee's head. Stitch 2 antennae protruding from the top of the circle and end each one with a French knot. At the tip of the longest finger, use straight stitches to make a "Y" with a short stem to indicate the stinger.

3. Glue the googly eyes in place.

4. Using the bee wing pattern on page 33, cut 2 ovals from black tulle.

5. Pinch the 2 tulle ovals together in the middle and sew them to the top of the bee's body with black sewing thread.

6. Trim the square to 8½" x 8½", making sure that the handprint is centered.

Constructing the Pillow

1. Sew the 2½" x 8½" bee-print inner-border strips to the sides of the block. Press the seams toward the border. Sew the 2½" x 12½" bee-print inner-border strips to the top and bottom edges of the block. Press the seams toward the border.

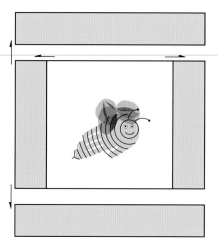

2. Sew the 2½" x 12½" sunflower-print outer-border strips to the sides of the pillow front. Press the seams toward the border. Sew the 2½" x 16½" sunflower-print outer-border strips to the top and bottom edges of the pillow front. Press the seams toward the border. The pillow front should now measure 16½" x 16½".

3. Layer the quilt batting on top of the 18" x 18" muslin square. Place the pillow front right side up on the batting. Pin the layers together.

4. Sew black rickrack around the handprint block, centering the trim on the seam between the block and the bee-print border. Quilt along the other seam lines of the layered pillow top. Trim the batting and backing even with the edges of the pillow front.

5. Sew black rickrack along the edges of your pillow top, centering the trim ¼" from the raw edges as shown on page 10. It is easier to cut a separate piece of rickrack for each side than to try and go around the corners with one long piece. For neat corners, make sure that the rickrack tapers off (ends with a valley rather than a hump) at the corners.

6. Press one long edge of each 12" x 16½" sunflower-print piece under by ¼". Press each fold under ¼" again and stitch along the inner folds. These 2 pieces make up the pillow back.

7. With right sides together, place one pillow back piece over the pillow front. Match raw edges of pillow back

to pillow front (not muslin). Place the second piece on top, overlapping the first. Pin in place.

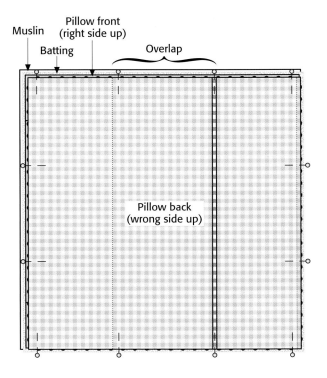

Muslin · Pillow front (right side up) · Batting · Overlap · Pillow back (wrong side up)

8. With the muslin side up, stitch around the pillow, using the rickrack stitching line as a guide. After the stitching is complete, trim the seams and clip across corners. Turn the pillow cover right side out and insert the pillow form.

Design Tip
Use any of the handprint designs in this book to make a charming pillow. Simply substitute a different block design for the Bee block. If the block size differs from this one, adjust your borders accordingly or make a smaller or a larger pillow.

Something Fishy

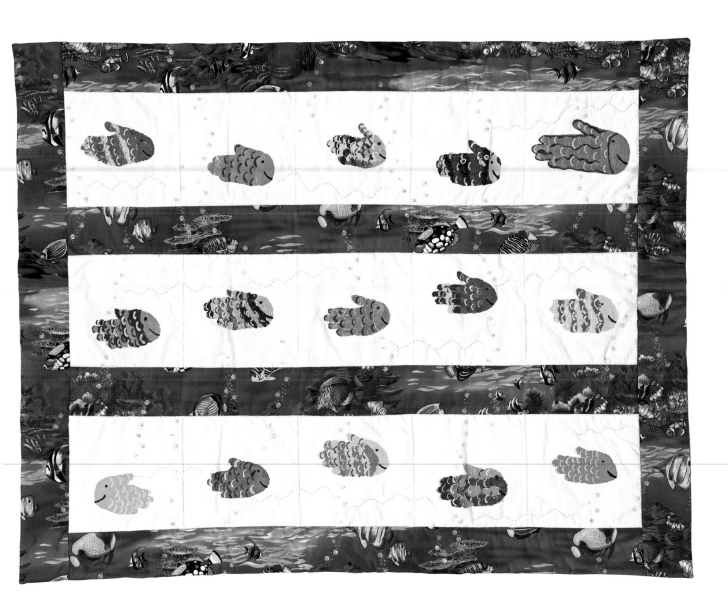

By Marcia L. Layton, 47" x 38". Printed by Sue Johnston and her class of three-year-olds
at Play Haven Preschool, Tampa, Florida. (From the collection of the Rogers family.)

*A lovely blue undersea print is the perfect border for a school
of bright, colorful fish and shiny sequin bubbles.*

Materials

Yardage is based on 42"-wide fabric.

1¾ yds. of muslin for blocks

1¾ yds. of sea print for sashing and borders

1⅝ yds. of fabric for backing

42" x 51" piece of low-loft batting

Acrylic paint: aqua, black, light blue, royal blue, fuchsia, lime green, moss green, lavender, orange, purple, red, and yellow

Red and blue glittery dimensional paint

Green and gold iridescent dimensional paint

8 mm iridescent sequins (about 200)

10/0 clear glass seed beads (about 200)

Light blue hand-quilting thread

Fabric	Pieces to Cut
Muslin	15 squares, 10½" x 10½"
Sea print	4 strips, 4" x 40½" 2 strips, 4" x 38½" (cut on the lengthwise grain)
Backing	42" x 51"

Making the Handprint Blocks

Refer to "Printing the Quilt" on page 6. Use the photo on page 37 as a guide for placement of the different embellishments.

1. Using just 1 color or a combination of 2 or more colors, create a handprint on a square of muslin. (Refer to the photo for ideas on color combinations.) Print the hand in the center of the square with all of the fingers held close together. Print a total of 14 squares with the left hand and 1 square with the right. Heat-set the handprints, following the manufacturer's directions.

Note: The handprints are printed with the fingers pointing up and away from the printer. After printing, the squares are turned sideways.

2. Turn the squares to the side so that the thumbs of each print are on top. Paint the eyes, mouth, and scales of each fish with dimensional paint. Each fish head covers part of the palm, and the scales go across the hand and fingers.

3. Arrange the squares in 3 rows of 5 fish each, positioning the fish for balanced color throughout. Place the right-handed fish print at the bottom left of the bottom row of fish.

4. Trim the squares to 8½" x 8½". Instead of centering each print within the square as you normally would, stagger the positions of the fish in each row. Trim more or less off the top and bottom edges of each square to move the fish up or down in relation to the other fish in its row.

Constructing the Quilt

All measurements include ¼"-wide seam allowances unless otherwise noted.

1. Sew each row of 5 fish together to make a total of 3 long panels.

Make 3.

2. Sew 2 of the 4" x 40½" sea-print sashing strips between the fish panels. Press the seams toward the sashing.

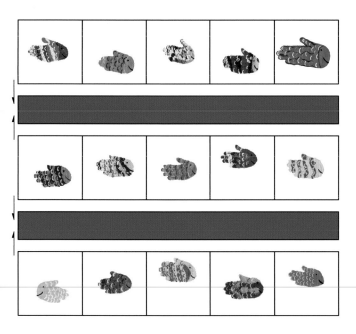

3. Sew two 4" x 40½" sea-print border strips to the top and bottom of the quilt top. Press the seams toward the border. Sew the 4" x 38½" sea-print border strips to the sides of the quilt top. Press the seams toward the border.

4. Create bubbles by sewing sequins to the quilt, anchoring each one in place with a bead as shown at top right. Position some "bubbles" on the border fabric and let them travel up over the fish panels.

(Refer to the quilt photo on page 37 for placement.) It's not necessary to knot off and cut the thread after every sequin. Instead, make a knot on the underside of the fabric at the beginning and at each sequin. Carry the thread across the back of the quilt top between sequins. Be sure to keep your fabric flat as you attach the sequins.

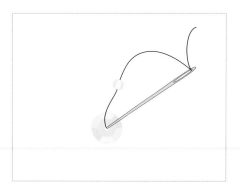

5. This quilt has no binding. (With this particular fabric, I didn't want anything to distract from the border.) To finish the quilt, construct the quilt sandwich following "Finishing with Rickrack Edging" on page 10, but omit the rickrack. Machine quilt along the seam lines.

6. Referring to the photo, use light blue hand-quilting thread to quilt blue "waves" across each fish panel, running them right across the seams that join the handprint squares. Add a label to the back of the quilt.

Design Tip

With this quilt, I really wanted to print the fish as a panel, but I was afraid to risk it because the fish were complicated to print and the children were very young. One misprint would have ruined a whole panel, but rows of individual blocks with sashing would have made the quilt much too wide. I solved the problem by printing individual blocks and joining them directly, without sashing. Quilting across the seams helped to bring the block panels together.

Dalmatians Everywhere!

By Marcia L. Layton, 38" x 45". Printed by Ruth Toro and her class of two-year-olds at Play Haven Preschool, Tampa, Florida. (From the collection of the Tini family.)

Twelve black-and-white Dalmatians are framed with yellow ribbon ladders and a bright red Dalmatian print.

Materials

Yardage is based on 42"-wide fabric.

2⅝ yds. of red Dalmatian print for outside border and backing

1⅝ yds. of muslin for blocks

½ yd. of spotted print for sashing and inner border

42" x 49" piece of low-loft batting

Acrylic paints: black and white

Black embroidery floss

Fabric glue

12 pairs of 3 mm googly eyes

2½ yds. of ¼"-wide blue ribbon

1⅛ yds. of ¼"-wide white ribbon with black spots

4¼ yds. of 1"-wide golden yellow ribbon

6½ yds. of 1¼"-wide golden yellow ribbon

4⅞ yds. of black rickrack, medium sized

Fabric	Pieces to Cut
Muslin	12 rectangles, 10½" x 11½" 6 rectangles, 3" x 9½"
Spotted print	4 strips, 2" x 37½" 2 strips, 2" x 33½"
Dalmatian print	2 strips, 3" x 40½" 2 strips, 3" x 38½" 1 piece, 42" x 49"

Making the Handprint Blocks

Refer to "Printing the Quilt" on page 6 and "Embellishing the Quilt" on pages 7–8. Use the quilt photo on page 40 as a guide for placement of the embroidery stitches and embellishments. Refer to the embroidery stitches on page 8, and use 2 strands of embroidery floss for the stitches.

1. For each Dalmatian, paint the printer's hand with a base of white paint, and then add black spots (I used both left and right handprints in my quilt). Print the hand approximately in the center of a 10½" x 11½" rectangle of muslin, keeping the 11½" edges along the top and bottom, with the fingers slightly spread and the thumb extended. Print a total of 12 rectangles. Turn the prints upside down. Heat-set the handprints, following the manufacturer's directions.

2. Using the detail photo below as a guide, use black embroidery floss and a backstitch to embroider the dog's ears and around its head (the thumb). Use a running stitch and black embroidery floss to continue stitching around the handprint. (This gives some definition to the mostly white dog's body, and it mimics its spots.)

3. To finish up the dog's face, fill in a small triangle with a satin stitch to make a nose and use straight stitches to make a small mouth just below the nose.

4. Embroider toes on the dog's paws with a straight stitch.

5. Glue 2 googly eyes in place.

6. Cut a 6" to 7" length of blue ribbon. Tie the ribbon into a bow and glue it to the dog's neck.

7. Cut a 3" piece of white ribbon with black spots. Make a tail by gluing this ribbon in place at the desired angle at the base of the palm.

8. Repeat steps 2–7 to make a total of 12 rectangles with Dalmatian prints. Vary the angle of the tail on each print to match the personality of the dog.

9. Trim the rectangles to 8½" long x 9½" wide.

Constructing the Quilt

All the measurements include ¼"-wide seam allowances unless otherwise noted.

1. Join 4 Dalmatian blocks as shown, adding a 3" x 9½" muslin rectangle to each end. Repeat to make 3 units.

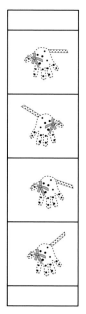

Make 3.

2. Cut fifteen 1" x 9½" pieces from the 1"-wide golden yellow ribbon. Center each piece over a horizontal seam, and glue the ribbon in place.

3. Align one long edge of the 1¼"-wide golden yellow ribbon with one long raw edge of a Dalmatian unit. Machine baste the outer edge, leaving the inner edge free. Repeat for all long edges of the Dalmatian units.

4. Sew 2 of the 2" x 37½" spotted-print sashing strips between the 3 block "ladders." Press the seams toward the sashing.

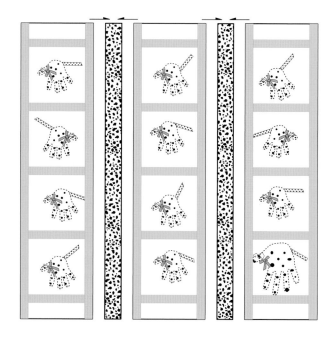

5. Sew two 2" x 37½" spotted-print inner-border strips to the sides of the quilt top. Press the seams toward the border.

6. Glue the unsewn inner edges of the 1¼"-wide golden yellow ribbon to the Dalmatian blocks.

7. Sew the 2" x 33½" spotted inner-border strips to the top and bottom of the quilt top. Press the seams toward the border.

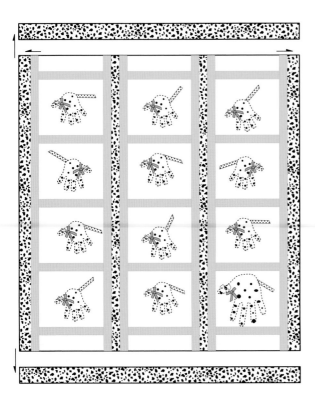

8. Sew the 3" x 40½" Dalmatian-print outer-border strips to the sides of the quilt top. Press the seams toward the border. Sew the 3" x 38½" Dalmatian-print outer-border strips to the top and bottom of the quilt top. Press the seams toward the border.

9. Refer to "Finishing with Rickrack Edging" on page 10 to construct the quilt sandwich and finish the quilt, using the black rickrack. Machine quilt along the seam lines. Add a label to the back of the quilt.

Design Tip

If you like things very precise, you could print the Dalmatians solid white and add the spots afterward with dimensional paint.

The choice of 1¼"-wide yellow ribbon for the long sides of the ladders in this quilt actually was the result of my running out of the 1"-wide yellow ribbon I used for the rungs. After searching area stores for the ribbon width I needed, with no success, I realized that I could sew part of the wider ribbon into the seam and make it match. That actually turned out to be a better way to secure the ribbon ladder to the quilt top! Don't panic if you come to a problem. You'll often find a solution that's better than your original plan.

Dinosaur Days

By Marcia L. Layton, 46" x 43½". Printed by Betsy Sanders and her class of three-year-olds at Play Haven Preschool, Tampa, Florida. (From the collection of Betsy Sanders.)

The border fabric was the inspiration for these printed panels of dinosaurs and palm trees.

Materials

Yardage is based on 42"-wide fabric.

1¾ yds. of dinosaur print for sashing and outer border

1⅛ yds. of muslin for printed panels

¼ yd. of fuchsia print for side inner borders

⅛ yd. *each* of blue, yellow, green, and orange prints for sashing and inner border

2 yds. of fabric for backing

½ yd. of red print for binding

47½" x 50" piece of low-loft batting

Acrylic paints: blue, fuchsia, green, orange, red, and yellow

Dimensional fabric paints: blue, green, orange, red, and yellow

½ yd. of ⅝"-wide yellow ribbon

¼ yd. *each* of ⅝"-wide purple and orange ribbons

Green embroidery floss

Fabric glue

1¼ yds. *each* of medium-sized yellow and medium-sized green rickrack

¾ yd. of medium-sized blue rickrack

⅝ yd. *each* of large-sized yellow, small-sized purple, and small-sized orange rickrack

⅜ yd. *each* of large-sized orange, medium-sized red, and small-sized red rickrack

Ten 3 mm googly eyes

Light blue hand-quilting thread

Fabric	Pieces to Cut
Muslin	2 rectangles, 17½" x 40"
Green print	1 strip, 1¾" x 38"
Orange print	1 strip, 1¾" x 38"
Yellow print	1 strip, 1¾" x 38"
Blue print	1 strip, 1¾" x 38"
Dinosaur print	1 strip, 3" x 38" 2 strips, 3¼" x 40½" 2 strips, 3¼" x 43½" (cut on the lengthwise grain)
Fuchsia print	2 strips, 1¾" x 38"
Backing	1 piece, 47½" x 50"
Red	5 strips, 2" x 42"

Making the Handprint Panels

Refer to "Printing the Quilt" on page 6 and "Embellishing the Quilt" on pages 7–8. Use the photo on page 44 as a guide for placement of the embroidery stitches and embellishments. Refer to the embroidery stitches on page 8 and use 3 strands of embroidery floss for the stitches.

1. To determine the placement of the handprints, use pins to mark the centers of the muslin panels along each edge. Also place a pin at each corner 1" in from the sides to mark off the trimmed panel dimensions (15½" x 38"). The extra inches in your panels allow you some room for adjustment if you do get things off-center while printing. Practice putting hands on the fabric and place pins to mark where the prints should go. You will print 5 dinosaurs and 2 palm trees evenly spaced across each of the 2 panels.

2. Print the palm trees first. Paint the printer's hand green and create a handprint with the fingers slightly spread. Print the 2 short palm trees (see photo on page 44) with the hand straight up and the 2 tall trees with the hand tilted slightly. Print a right hand and a left hand on each panel. Turn each panel upside down.

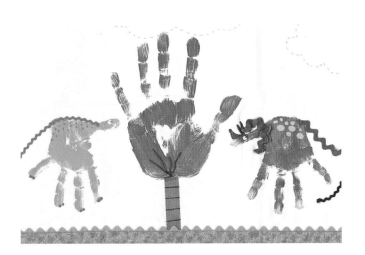

3. There are 3 kinds of dinosaurs on the quilt—1 long-necked (apatosaurus), 1 three-horned (triceratops), and 1 spike-tailed (stegosaurus). Print them all in the same manner, using both right and left handprints, with the fingers spread and the thumb extended. Extend the thumb as far as it will go for the long-necked dinosaur. Refer to the quilt photo for the color and placement of each print. Print the dinosaurs at the tops of the panels. The fingertips should be placed about 2" below the raw edge of the fabric. When the printing is complete, turn the panels right side up and heat-set the handprints, following the manufacturer's directions.

4. To embellish the palm trees, glue lengths of ⅝"-wide ribbon from the bottoms of the handprints to the edges of the panels. (See the photo for ribbon color placement.) Then use green embroidery floss to couch the ribbon, placing stitches about ½" apart. At the base of each handprint, make 4 long straight stitches across the palm with the green floss.

5. To embellish each long-necked dinosaur, glue a 7" length of small- or medium-sized rickrack in a curve from the tip of the thumb, across the edge of the palm, and down. Extend the rickrack away from the handprint to make a tail at the end. (See the photo on page 44 for color and placement ideas.) Use dimensional paint to add 2 dots to the tips of each fingerprint to make toes on the dinosaur's feet. If desired, add spots to the dinosaur's back with dimensional paint. Glue 1 googly eye in place on each dinosaur.

6. To embellish each three-horned dinosaur, fold and glue a 9" piece of medium-sized rickrack in half, making a double wave. Glue the wavy piece in a

curve at the base of the dinosaur's head (the thumbprint) for its bony frill. Glue a 3" piece of the same medium-sized rickrack to the dinosaur's back (the edge of the palm) for its tail. Use yellow dimensional-paint to add 3 dots to the tips of each fingerprint to make toes on the dinosaur's feet. Add yellow dimensional paint spots to the dinosaur's back. Use blue dimensional paint to add 3 horns to each dinosour's head. Glue 1 googly eye in place on each dinosaur.

7. To embellish each spike-tailed dinosaur, glue a 9" piece of large-sized rickrack from the base of the thumb, along the edge of the palm, and down to form a tail. Pinch parts of the rickrack together to make it stand out from the fabric. This represents the bony plates on the dinosaur's back and the spikes on its tail. Fold the rickrack back under itself at the end of the tail. Use dimensional paint to add 2 dots to the tips of each fingerprint to make toes on the dinosaur's feet. Add spots to the dinosaur's back with dimensional paint. Glue 1 googly eye in place on each dinosaur.

8. Trim the panels to 15½" x 38", centering the designs.

Constructing the Quilt

All measurements include ¼"-wide seam allowances unless otherwise noted.

1. Sew a piece of medium green rickrack to the bottom of the top panel, centering it ¼" from the raw edge as shown on page 10. Sew the 1¾" x 38" green sashing strip to the bottom of the panel, using the stitching line from the rickrack as a guide. Sew the 1¾" x 38" orange inner-border strip to the top edge of the panel. Press the seams toward the sashing and border.

2. Sew a piece of medium yellow rickrack to the bottom of the bottom panel, centering it ¼" from the raw edge as shown on page 10. Sew a 1¾" x 38" yellow inner-border strip to the bottom edge of the panel, using the stitching line from the rickrack as a guide. Sew a 1¾" x 38" blue sashing strip to the top of the panel. Press the seams toward the sashing and border.

3. Sew the 3" x 38" dinosaur-print sashing strip between the 2 printed panels. Press the seams toward the sashing.

4. Sew the 1¾" x 38" fuchsia border strips to the sides of the quilt top. Press the seams toward the border.

5. Sew the 3¼" x 40½" dinosaur-print outer-border strips to the top and bottom of the quilt top. Press the seams toward the border. Join the 3¼" x 43½" dinosaur-print outer-border strips to the sides of the quilt top. Press the seams toward the border.

6. Referring to "Finishing with Binding" on page 9, construct the quilt sandwich, pin-baste, and machine quilt along the seam lines.

7. Transfer the cloud patterns on pages 48–50 to paper and cut them out on the lines. Position cloud patterns 1–4 from right to left across the top of the top panel, using the project photo as a guide, and pin them in place. Repeat on the bottom panel, using clouds 5–9. With light blue hand-quilting thread, quilt around the cloud patterns. Remove the patterns.

8. Bind the edges of the quilt and add a label to the back of the quilt.

Design Tip

Printing these dinosaurs in darker colors and combining them with fabrics that imitate nature could make this quilt appeal to an older child. A background with painted or embroidered jungle ferns and grasses, or even a volcano, could really make this dinosaur world come alive!

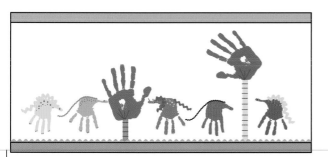

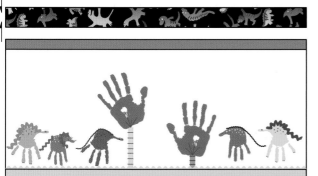

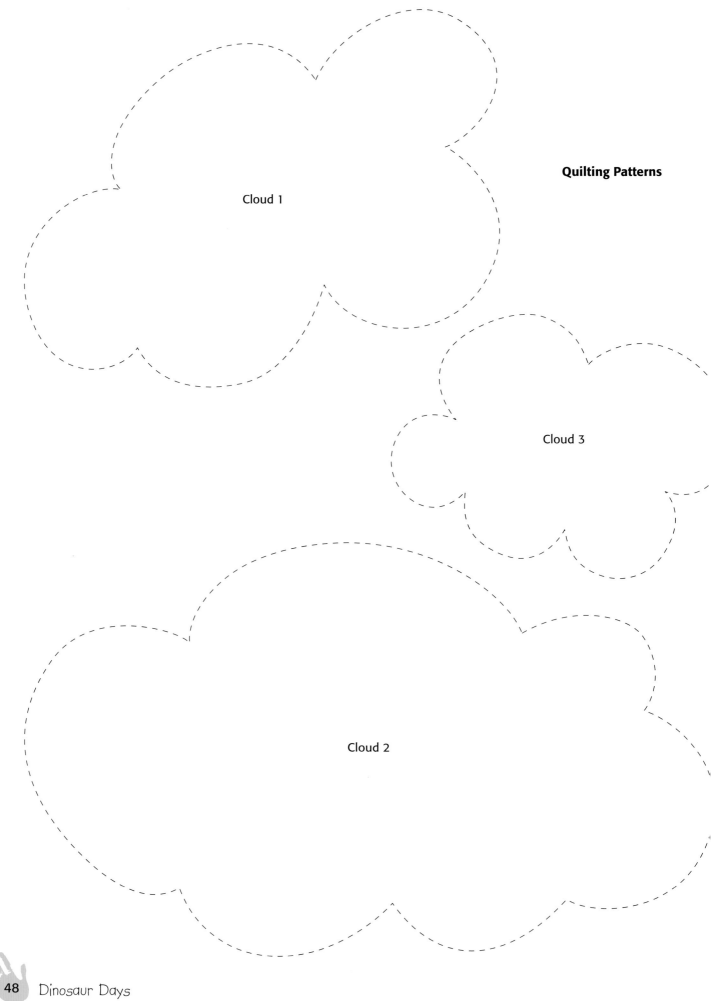

Quilting Patterns

Cloud 1

Cloud 3

Cloud 2

Quilting Patterns

Cloud 4

Cloud 5

Cloud 6

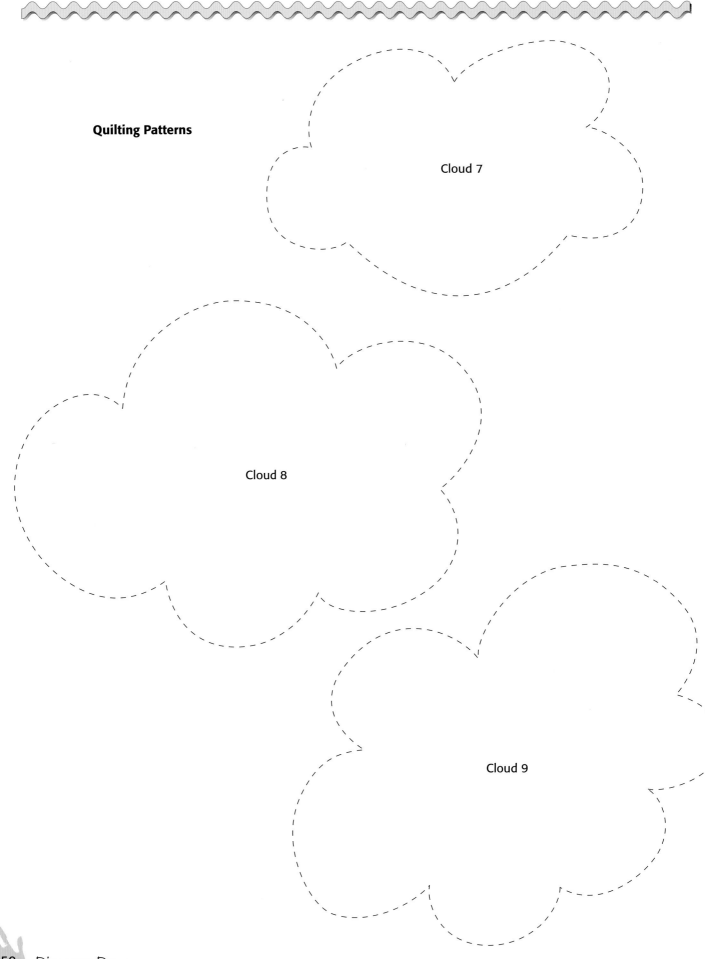

Quilting Patterns

Cloud 7

Cloud 8

Cloud 9

Jungle Rumble

By Marcia L. Layton, 29½" x 29½". Printed by four-year-olds
at Play Haven Preschool, Tampa, Florida.

*Little hands come to life as a zebra, lion, elephant, and giraffe
in this small jungle quilt, perfect for a young child's room.*

Materials

Yardage is based on 42"-wide fabric.

¾ yd. of animal print for outer border

½ yd. of muslin for blocks

¼ yd. of yellow check for sashing

¼ yd. of green check for inner border

1⅜ yds. of spotted print for binding and backing

34" x 34" square of low-loft batting

Acrylic paints: black, brown, gray, tan, white, and golden yellow

Embroidery floss: black, brown, gray, pink, white, pale yellow, and green

Fabric glue

Six 3 mm googly eyes

Two 5 mm brown pompoms

5" length of loopy-textured polyester fringe

Two 10 mm tan pompoms

Fabric	Pieces to Cut
Muslin	4 squares, 10½" x 10½"
Yellow check	2 strips, 2" x 8½" 1 strip, 2" x 18"
Green check	2 strips, 2" x 18" 2 strips, 2" x 21"
Animal print	2 strips, 4¾" x 21" 2 strips, 4¾" x 29½"
Spotted print	4 strips, 2" x 42" 1 square, 34" x 34"

Making the Handprint Blocks

Refer to "Printing the Quilt" on page 6 and "Embellishing the Quilt" on pages 7–8. Use the quilt photo on page 51 as a guide for placement of the embroidery stitches and embellishments. Refer to the embroidery stitches on page 8 and use 3 strands of embroidery floss for the stitches unless otherwise directed.

Elephant

1. Use gray paint to create a handprint on a square of muslin; print the hand with the fingers slightly spread and the thumb extended. Turn the print upside down and heat-set the handprint, following the manufacturer's directions.
2. Use gray embroidery floss and a backstitch to embroider the elephant's ear. Make 2 French knots at the end of the thumbprint for the nostrils and 3 French knots at the end of each fingerprint for the toes.
3. Cut three 5"-long pieces of 6-strand gray embroidery floss for the tail. Knot 1 end of each 6-strand piece. Thread the unknotted end of 1 piece onto a needle and, at the desired starting point for the elephant's tail, bring the needle through the fabric from the back side. Repeat with the remaining 2 pieces. Braid the 3 strands together to the desired length. Tie another small piece of floss around the end of the braid to secure it, and cut off any excess length.
4. Use pink embroidery floss and a backstitch to embroider the elephant's mouth.
5. Glue 1 googly eye in place.

Giraffe

1. Paint the printer's hand with a base of golden yellow paint, and then add brown spots. Print the hand on a square of muslin with the fingers slightly spread and the thumb extended. Turn the print upside down and heat-set the handprint, following the manufacturer's directions.
2. Use brown embroidery floss and a backstitch to embroider the giraffe's ears and horns. Make 2 French knots at the end of the thumbprint for the nostrils.
3. Glue a brown pompom to the top of each horn.
4. Using brown embroidery floss, sew a row of running stitches for the giraffe's mane, and then sew a

second row of running stitches in the other direction, filling in the spaces as shown.

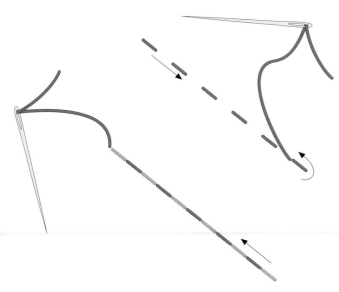

Make running stitches for mane.

5. Thread a 6-strand piece of brown embroidery floss on a needle. Thread the floss up and back down through one of the running stitches, making a loop. Clip the thread 1" away, and then pull the cut ends through the loop to make fringe as shown. Repeat at each running stitch. Trim the fringe evenly and separate the floss strands to fluff it out.

1. Make loop.   2. Pull thread ends through.   3. Clip threads.

Knotted Mane

6. Cut two 6-strand pieces of pale yellow embroidery floss and one 6-strand piece of brown floss, each 5" long, for the tail. Knot 1 end of each 6-strand piece. Thread the unknotted end of 1 piece onto a needle and, at the desired starting point for the giraffe's tail, bring the needle through the fabric from the back side. Repeat for the remaining 2 pieces. Braid the 3 pieces together to the desired length. Tie another small piece of floss around the end of the braid to secure it, and cut off any excess length.

7. Glue 2 googly eyes in place.

Zebra

1. Paint the printer's hand with a base of white paint. Add black vertical stripes on the palm, horizontal stripes on the fingers, and angled stripes on the thumb, as shown. Print the hand on a square of muslin, with the fingers slightly spread and the thumb extended. Turn the print upside down and heat-set the handprint, following the manufacturer's directions.

2. Use a French knot and black embroidery floss to embroider a nostril.

3. Sew a row of running stitches for the zebra's mane using black embroidery floss, as shown at left. Then stitch a second row of running stitches in the other direction, filling in the spaces and using white embroidery floss.

4. Thread a 6-strand piece of black embroidery floss on a needle. Thread the floss up and back down through one of the black running stitches, making a loop. Clip the thread 1" away, and then pull the cut ends through the loop to make fringe as shown at left. Repeat at each running stitch, matching the floss for the fringe to the color of the running stitch. Trim the fringe evenly and separate the floss strands to fluff it out.

5. Cut two 6-strand pieces of white embroidery floss and one 6-strand piece of black embroidery floss, each 5" long, for the tail. Knot 1 end of each 6-strand piece. Thread the unknotted end of 1 piece onto a needle and, at the desired starting point for the zebra's tail, bring the needle through the fabric from the back side. Repeat with the remaining 2 pieces. Braid the 3 pieces together to the desired length. Tie another small piece of floss around the end of the braid to secure it, and cut off any excess length.

6. Glue 1 googly eye in place.

Lion

1. Use tan paint to create a handprint on a square of muslin; print the hand with the fingers slightly

spread and the thumb extended. Turn the print upside down and heat-set the handprint, following the manufacturer's directions.

2. Use brown embroidery floss to embroider the lion's whiskers and mouth. Make 3 long, straight stitches, fanning out on each side of its face for its whiskers. Use a backstitch to form a small mouth. Make a French knot for the nose and embroider the claws on the feet with straight stitches.

3. Glue polyester fringe in a circle around the end of the thumbprint, centering the embroidered face in the circle. (For the mane, I left the bottom string that holds the fringe together intact and folded the fringe in half lengthwise before gluing it in place. This created a loopy texture.)

4. Unravel and cut six 5" lengths of thread from the polyester fringe. Using a needle threaded with sewing thread, sew across the fringe ends to secure them to the lion at the starting point for its tail. Separate the lengths into three 2-strand sections and braid the sections together to the desired length. Tie another small piece of thread from the polyester fringe around the end of the braid to secure it, and cut off any excess length.

5. Glue 2 googly eyes in place. Glue tan pompoms above the eyes for ears.

Grass

With green embroidery floss, embroider a line of running stitches across each block, curving the line above or below each animal's feet, as shown in the photo. Using the same knotted fringe technique as for the zebra and the giraffe's manes, make about 5 or 6 loops in the line of stitching to create tufts of grass.

Constructing the Quilt

All measurements include ¼"-wide seam allowances unless otherwise noted.

1. Trim the squares to 8½" x 8½".

2. Sew a 2" x 8½" yellow check sashing strip between the zebra and giraffe blocks. Press the seam allowances toward the sashing. Sew the second 2" x 8½" yellow check sashing strip between the lion and elephant blocks. Join the pairs of blocks

with the 2" x 18" yellow check sashing strip. Press the seams toward the sashing.

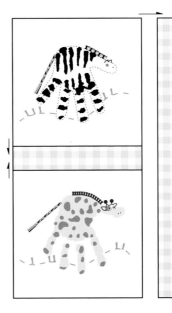

3. Sew the 2" x 18" green check inner-border strips to the sides of the quilt top. Press the seams toward the border. Sew the 2" x 21" green check inner-border strips to the top and bottom of the quilt. Press the seams toward the border.

4. Sew the 4¾" x 21" animal-print outer-border strips to the sides of the quilt top. Press the seams toward the border. Sew the 4¾" x 29½" animal-print outer-border strips to the top and bottom of the quilt top. Press the seams toward the border.

5. Referring to "Finishing with Binding" on page 9, construct the quilt sandwich, pin-baste, and machine quilt along the seam lines. Bind the edges of the quilt and add a label to the back.

Design Tip
Any one of the animals in this quilt could star in a quilt of its own. From tiny pink elephants combined with a pink gingham border to black-and-white zebras surrounded by a vivid jungle print, the possibilities are endless. These animals would also look great printed on a panel between palm-tree handprints. See the palm-tree handprints in "Dinosaur Days" on page 44.

Circus Fun

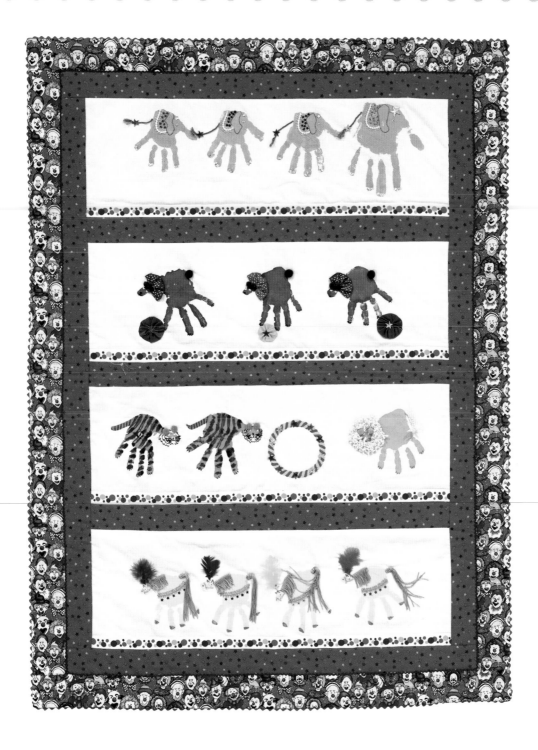

By Marcia L. Layton, 36½" x 51½". Printed by Marcia L. Layton and her class of four-year-olds at Play Haven Preschool, Tampa, Florida. (From the collection of the Lykes family.)

All the excitement of a circus parade is depicted in the panels of this sparkly quilt.

Materials

Yardage is based on 42"-wide fabric.

1½ yds. of muslin for printed panels

1½ yds. of circus print for outer border

1⅜ yds. of red print for sashing and inner border

1¾ yds. of fabric for backing

41" x 56" piece of low-loft batting

Acrylic paints: black, brown, cream, gray, orange, and tan

Embroidery floss: black, brown, gray, and pink

5 mm round silver sequins

Glass seed beads: blue, clear, gold, green, and red

Fabric glue

½ yd. of silver braid

3 mm and 16 mm star sequins in blue, gold, green, and red

20 googly eyes

One 22 mm and three 8 mm acrylic star jewels

¾ yd. of 1"-wide green ribbon

¾ yd. of ⅝"-wide yellow ribbon

⅜ yd. of 1"-wide red ribbon with white polka dots

½ yd. 1"-wide blue ribbon with white polka dots

3 brown 15 mm pompoms

6 brown, 2 tan, and 4 orange 10 mm pompoms

¼ yd. of ⅜"-wide orange ribbon

¼ yd. of beige loopy-textured polyester fringe

½ yd. of yellow rickrack, medium sized

5½ yds. of red rickrack, medium sized

½ yd. of gold fringe

Gold ribbon floss

Gold dimensional paint

Feathers: 1 blue, 1 green, 1 red, and 1 yellow

½ yd. of gold braid

3⅛ yds. of 1"-wide multicolor-print ribbon

4¼ yds. of green rickrack, small sized

Fabric	Pieces to Cut
Muslin	4 panels, 11½" x 29½"
Red print	3 strips, 2½" x 27½" 2 strips, 2½" x 42½" 2 strips, 2½" x 31½"
Circus print	2 strips, 3" x 46½" (cut on the lengthwise grain) 2 strips, 3" x 36½"
Backing	1 piece, 41" x 56"

Making the Handprint Panels

Refer to "Printing the Quilt" on page 6 and "Embellishing the Quilt" on pages 7–8. Use the quilt photo on page 55 as a guide for placement of the embroidery stitches and embellishments. Refer to the embroidery stitches on page 8 and use 3 strands of embroidery floss for the stitches unless otherwise directed.

To determine the placement of the handprints, use pins to mark the centers of the muslin panels along the top and bottom edges. Also place a pin at each corner 1" in from the sides to mark off the trimmed panel dimensions (9½" x 27½"). The extra inches in your panels allow you some room for adjustment if you do get things off-center while printing. For each panel, refer to the project photo on page 55 and practice placing hands on the fabric until you get a pleasing arrangement and even spacing. Place a pin just below the spot where you want each print to be.

Note: The handprints are printed with the fingers pointing up and away from the printer. After printing, each panel is turned upside down.

Elephants

1. Position 4 right handprints on a muslin panel, placing 2 prints on each side of the center pins. From left to right, position the tips of the large handprint about 3" below the raw edge of the panel. (This allows room for the ribbon border, attached later.) Position the smaller elephants lower, more in the center of the panel. Paint the printer's hands with gray paint. Print the hands, keeping the fingers spread apart and the thumb extended. Turn the

panel upside down and heat-set the handprints, following the manufacturer's directions.

2. Backstitch the elephants' ears with gray embroidery floss and their mouths with pink embroidery floss.

3. Sew 3 round silver sequins to the tip of each finger, anchoring each one with a bead, to make the elephants' toes.

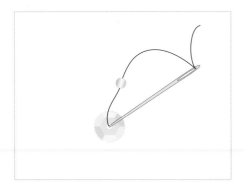

4. Glue a 3" piece of silver braid to the back of each elephant behind the ear. Use beads to anchor the 3 mm sequin stars in the space between the braid and the ear. Use a single color (red, blue, green, or gold) on each elephant.

5. Glue a googly eye in place on each elephant's head. Glue a 22 mm star jewel to the top of the head of the large elephant and 8 mm star jewels to the heads of the other 3 elephants.

6. Cut three 5"-long pieces of 6-strand gray embroidery floss for the tail. Knot 1 end of each piece. Thread the unknotted end of 1 piece onto a needle and, at the desired starting point for the elephant's tail, bring the needle through the fabric from the back side. Repeat with the remaining 2 pieces. Braid the 3 pieces together to the desired length. Tie another small piece of floss around the end of the braid to secure it, and cut off any excess length. Sew a 16 mm sequin star over the knot on each tail, anchoring each sequin with a bead. (Match the color of this star to the stars on each elephant's back.)

Bears

1. Position 3 left handprints along a muslin panel, printing the center handprint in the center of the panel and spacing the other 2 evenly on each side. Paint the printer's hands brown and print the handprints on the fabric with the fingers spread and the thumb extended, positioned about 4½" from the upper raw edge of the panel. Turn the printed panel upside down and heat-set the handprints, following the manufacturer's directions.

2. Cut two 11" pieces of green ribbon and one 11" piece of yellow ribbon. With a threaded needle, hand-gather 1 edge of 1 ribbon and pull the thread to create a circle. Tie the thread in a knot, tuck under the ends of the ribbon, and secure with glue. Repeat for the other 2 ribbons. Glue the ribbon "balls" to the panel just below the bears' feet. Sew a 16 mm star sequin to the center of each ball, anchoring it with a bead.

3. Cut one 6½" length of red polka-dotted ribbon and two 6½" lengths of blue polka-dotted ribbon. With a threaded needle, gather 1 edge of each ribbon to create a ruffle for each bear's neck. Knot the thread at each end and tuck under the ends; secure with glue. Glue a ruffle across the base of each thumbprint, as shown in the photo below.

4. Glue a 15 mm brown pompom to the upper right of the handprint palm for each bear's tail. Glue two 10 mm brown pompoms to each thumb for ears. Embroider a tiny black French knot at the tip of each thumb for a nose. Embroider black claws with straight stitches at the tip of each finger.

5. Glue 2 googly eyes to each bear's face.

Tigers, Lion, and Ring

1. To print the tigers, paint 2 right hands with a base of orange paint, and then add black vertical stripes on the palm, horizontal stripes on the fingers, and angled stripes on the thumb, as shown below. Print the hands to the right of the center pin on a muslin panel, with the fingers spread and the thumb extended, about 4" below the upper raw edge of the panel.

2. To print the lion, paint a printer's left hand with tan paint and print the hand the same distance from the center pin as the tiger on the far right, with the fingers spread and the thumb extended. Make sure it's printed about 4" below the upper raw edge of the panel.

3. Turn the panel upside down and heat-set the handprints, following the manufacturer's directions.

4. Use black embroidery floss and backstitches to embroider fur around the tigers' faces (the thumbs). Add mouths and whiskers with straight stitches and make French knots for the noses. Embroider the claws on the feet with straight stitches.

5. Glue 2 orange 10 mm pompoms to each tiger's face for the ears. Glue 2 googly eyes in place on each tiger. Glue a 2" to 3" piece of orange ribbon to the left side of each tiger (the palm) for the tails. Couch the tails with black embroidery floss.

6. To embellish the lion, see page 54 and follow steps 2–5.

7. To form the ring between the tigers and lion, twist two 16"-long pieces of yellow and red rickrack together to form a circle. (The diameter of the circle should be about 4½".) Glue the circle in place, concealing the rickrack's raw edges with a sequin star. Sew red, green, gold, and blue 16 mm sequin stars to the ring, anchoring them with beads.

Ponies

1. Paint a printer's left hand with cream paint and print with the fingers spread and the thumb extended. Position 4 left handprints across a muslin panel, placing the fingertips about 3" below the top raw edge of the panel. Turn the panel upside down and heat-set the handprints, following the manufacturer's directions.

2. Cut a 2½" piece of gold fringe for each pony's mane. Fold the top edge of the trim in half and secure with glue. Glue this edge to the top of the thumb and palm, tucking the ends under and securing them with glue. Trim the fringe to about 1" long. Cut a 1" piece of fringe for each tail. Roll the fringe heading tightly around itself, securing with glue as you go to make a tight coil. Glue the coiled end to the upper right of the palm.

3. Use brown embroidery floss and straight stitches to embroider ears on the thumbprint faces and to create each nostril using a French knot. Glue a googly eye in place on each pony's head. Use gold ribbon floss to stitch a halter across the thumb. Also wrap gold ribbon floss around the top of each pony's tail. Use gold dimensional paint to add the hooves at the end of each finger.

4. Glue a blue, green, red, or yellow feather to the top of each pony's head and attach a matching 16 mm sequin star to the bottom of each feather, anchoring the stars with beads as before for the elephants. Glue a 4" piece of gold braid across the palms and attach 3 mm sequin stars, matching the feathers along the braid, anchoring the stars with beads as before.

Constructing the Quilt

All measurements include ¼"-wide seam allowances unless otherwise noted.

1. Trim the panels to 9½" x 27½", centering your circus animals. Sew three 2½" x 27½" red print sashing strips between the panels. Press seam allowances toward the sashing.

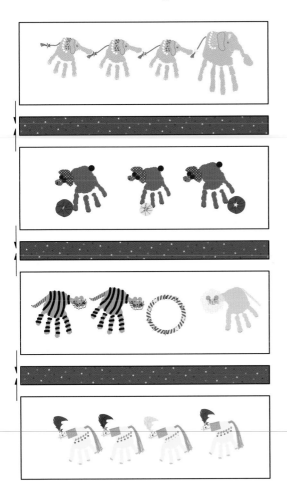

2. Just above the seam line at the bottom of each panel, glue a length of multicolor-print ribbon to the muslin.

3. Sew the 2½" x 42½" red print inner-border strips to the sides of the quilt top. Press the seams toward the border. Sew the 2½" x 31½" red print inner-border strips to the top and bottom of the quilt top,

being careful not to catch the multicolor ribbon in the seam allowance at the bottom. Press the seams toward the border.

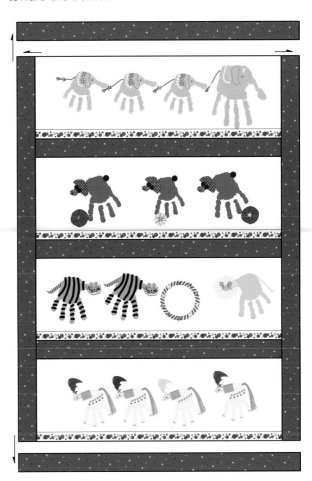

4. Sew the 3" x 46½" circus-print outer-border strips to the sides of the quilt top. Press the seams toward the outer border. Sew the 3" x 36½" outer-border strips to the top and bottom of the quilt top. Press the seams toward the outer border.

5. Referring to "Finishing with Rickrack Edging" on page 10, construct the quilt sandwich and finish the quilt, using the red rickrack.

6. Sew the small green rickrack over the seam between the inner and outer borders. Machine quilt along the remaining seam lines and add a label to the back of the quilt.

Just Us Chickens

By Marcia L. Layton, 31" x 42". Printed by four-year-olds at Play Haven Preschool, Tampa, Florida.

Barnyard fowl peek out through "windows" in the sparkly gold chicken-wire background of this quilt.

Materials

Yardage is based on 42"-wide fabric.

¾ yd. of muslin for blocks

¾ yd. of gold lamé mesh for blocks

⅝ yd. of chicken print for sashing and inner border

½ yd. of red check for outer border

1⅝ yds. of dark red fabric for binding and backing

35" x 46" piece of low-loft batting

Acrylic paints: black, light brown, dark brown, medium brown, gold, gray, off-white, red, white, and yellow

Dimensional fabric paints: black, dark brown, light brown, gray, orange, and yellow

Fabric glue

Six 3 mm googly eyes

Gem-Tac

Fabric	Pieces to Cut
Muslin	6 squares, 10½" x 10½"
Gold lamé mesh	6 squares, 10½" x 10½"
Chicken print	4 strips, 3½" x 8½"
	3 strips, 3½" x 30½"
	2 strips, 3½" x 25½"
Red check	2 strips, 3¼" x 36½"
	2 strips, 3¼" x 31"
Dark red	4 strips, 2" x 42"
	1 piece, 35" x 46"

Making the Handprint Blocks

Refer to "Printing the Quilt" on page 6. Use the quilt photo on page 60 as a guide for placement of the embellishments.

1. Print 1 handprint in the center of each muslin square, with the fingers just slightly spread and angled slightly to the right and the thumbs extended. To print the 5 hens: Paint 1 hand with medium brown paint, dabbed with dark brown spots; 1 hand with gray paint, dabbed with black paint; 1 hand with light brown paint, blended with areas of yellow paint; 1 hand with gold paint, blended with areas of brown paint; and 1 hand with white paint, blended with areas of gray paint. For the rooster, paint 1 hand with 3 distinct areas of red, black, and brown.

2. Print tiny red fingerprints above and below the thumbs for the combs and wattles of the hens and rooster. Heat-set the handprints, following the manufacturer's directions.

3. Referring to the quilt photo on page 60, add beaks to the chickens with orange dimensional paint. Use dimensional paint in coordinating colors to mark feathers on the handprint bodies. Add 2 feet to each chicken with light brown dimensional paint and use black dimensional paint for the tiny claws.

4. Glue 1 googly eye in place on each chicken's head.

5. Trim the squares to 8½" x 8½".

Constructing the Quilt

All measurements include ¼"-wide seam allowances unless otherwise noted.

1. Photocopy the circle pattern on page 63, enlarging or reducing to fit your handprints.

2. Center the circle pattern over each 10½" x 10½" gold lamé mesh square. With a rotary cutter, cut out and discard the circle.

3. Position each lamé square over a printed chicken block and pin the lamé in place. Use Gem-Tac to glue the inside edges of the mesh to each muslin block. Machine baste around the outside edges of the blocks and trim the edges of the mesh even with the muslin.

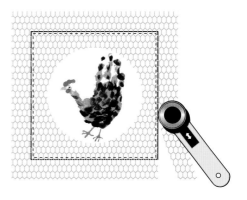

4. Sew two 3½" x 8½" chicken-print sashing strips between 3 blocks, referring to the photo for placement. Press the seams toward the sashing. Repeat to make 2 block and sashing units.

Make 2.

5. Join the 2 block and sashing units with a 3½" x 30½" chicken-print sashing strip. Press the seams toward the sashing.

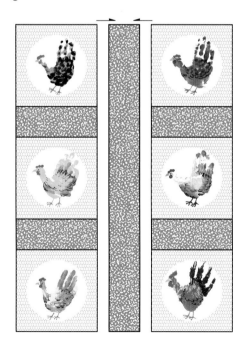

6. Sew the remaining 3½" x 30½" chicken-print inner border strips to the sides of the quilt top. Press the seams toward the border. Sew the 3½" x 25½" chicken-print inner border strips to the top and bot-

tom of the quilt top. Press the seams toward the border.

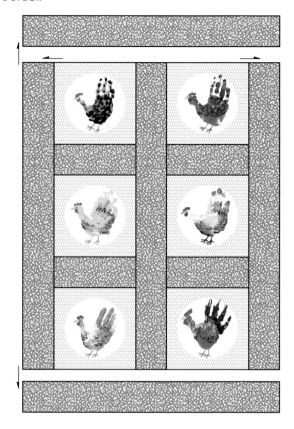

7. Sew the 3¼" x 36½" red outer border strips to the sides of the quilt top. Press the seams toward the border. Sew the 3¼" x 31" red outer border strips to the top and bottom of the quilt top. Press the seams toward the border.

8. Referring to "Finishing with Binding" on page 9, construct the quilt sandwich, pin-baste, and machine quilt along the seam lines. Bind the edges of the quilt and add a label to the back.

Design Tip

My original design called for the gold mesh to completely cover the handprint blocks. When I found that the chickens were lost behind the mesh, the idea for the circle cutouts came about. Sometimes, after you assemble all your fabrics and trims, new ideas will appear, so don't be afraid to have fun and experiment.

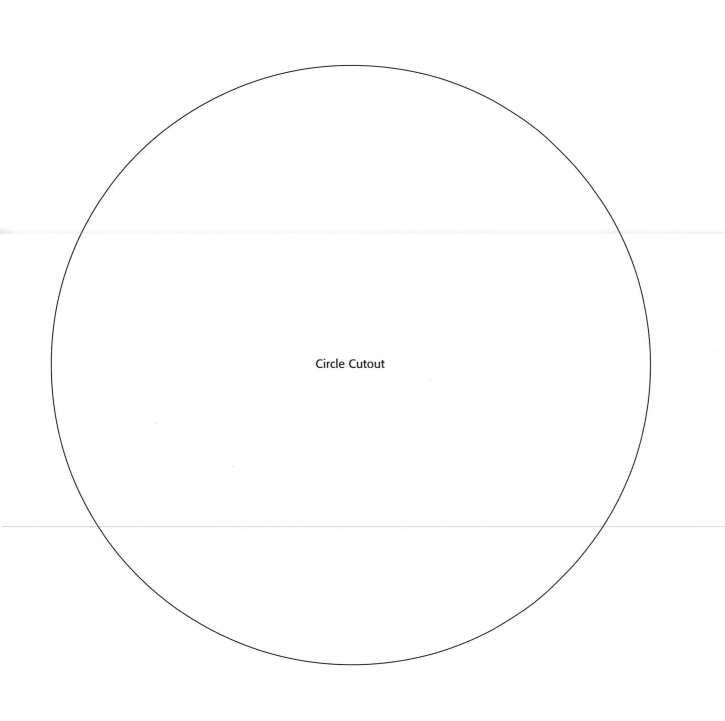

Circle Cutout

About the Author

Marcia Layton is a Florida native who spent much of her childhood traveling around the eastern United States and overseas to Germany and Australia with her Air Force family. She later attended Florida State University, where she graduated with a degree in French and German and a minor in art. It was during her college summers that she got her start working with young children as a performer and recreation counselor with the Florida State Flying High Circus at Callaway Gardens, Georgia. She has been teaching ever since. For the past 19 years, Marcia has been a pre-K teacher and assistant director of Play Haven Preschool in Tampa, Florida, where she teaches art, music, French, and school readiness skills to four-year-olds. Her handprint quilts have become an annual tradition at the school's spring art show and fund-raising event.

Inheriting a love of sewing from her grandmother and mother, she has always enjoyed experimenting with all kinds of arts and crafts, from painting to smocking to embroidery, and most recently, to quilting. She confesses to owning way too much fabric, having way too many unfinished projects sitting around, and spending way too much time looking at books for new projects to start!

She is the mother of four children, two of them grown, and she presently lives in Tampa with her two youngest children and two very pampered cats. Combining her passion for both sewing and teaching, this is her first book.